LECTURES AND CONVERSATIONS
on Aesthetics, Psychology and Religious Belief

L. WITTGENSTEIN

LECTURES & CONVERSATIONS

on Aesthetics, Psychology and Religious Belief

Compiled from Notes taken by Yorick Smythies, Rush Rhees and James Taylor

Edited by Cyril Barrett

UNIVERSITY OF CALIFORNIA PRESS

Berkeley and Los Angeles

University of California Press
Berkeley and Los Angeles, California

ISBN: 0–520–01354–9
Library of Congress Catalog Card Number: 66–19347
Printed in the United States of America

8 9 0

CONTENTS

PREFACE

The first thing to be said about this book is that nothing contained herein was written by Wittgenstein himself. The notes published here are not Wittgenstein's own lecture notes but notes taken down by students, which he neither saw nor checked. It is even doubtful if he would have approved of their publication, at least in their present form. Since, however, they deal with topics only briefly touched upon in his other published writings, and since for some time they have been circulating privately, it was thought best to publish them in a form approved by their authors.

The lectures on aesthetics were delivered in private rooms in Cambridge in the summer of 1938. They were given to a small group of students, which included Rush Rhees, Yorick Smythies, James Taylor, Casmir Lewy, Theodore Redpath and Maurice Drury (whose names occur in the text). The name of another student, Ursell, also occurs in the text (p. 28), but he did not attend the lectures. The lectures on religious belief belong to a course on belief given about the same time. The conversations on Freud between Wittgenstein and Rush Rhees took place between 1942 and 1946.

Besides the notes of the conversations on Freud, those of the fourth lecture on aesthetics are by Rush Rhees; the rest are by Smythies. Since we possess three versions of the first three lectures on aesthetics (by Smythies, Rhees and Taylor—referred to respectively as S, R, and T) and two versions of the fourth lecture, the most complete version has been chosen as the text and significant variants have been added in footnote. The notes have been printed as they were taken down at the time, except for some minor grammatical corrections and a few omissions where the original was indecipherable. Although the different versions agree to a remarkable extent, their authors do not vouch for their accuracy in every detail: they do not claim to give a verbatim report of what Wittgenstein said.

The inclusion of variants may give to what were, after all, no more than informal discussions, an importance and solemnity which may seem inappropriate. On the other hand, as should be clear, the different versions complement and clarify each other, and at the same time hint at their close agreement (which could be demonstrated only by printing all versions in full). It might have been possible to conflate the versions into a single text, but it seemed better to preserve each version as it was taken down and leave the reader to reconstruct a composite text for himself. At times, in the interests of clarity and smoother reading, some of the variants have been introduced into the text. Wherever this is done, and also where editorial emendations have been made, square brackets have been employed. The use of three dots (...) usually indicates that there is a lacuna or an indecipherable passage in the text.

Finally, a word about the choice of material. This is only a selection from the extant students' notes of Wittgenstein's lectures. Yet, in spite of appearances, it is not a random selection. The notes printed here reflect Wittgenstein's opinions on and attitude to life, to religious, psychological and artistic questions. That Wittgenstein himself did not keep these questions separate is clear, for example, from G. E. Moore's account of the 1930–33 lectures (*Mind* 1955).

C. B.

LECTURES ON AESTHETICS

I

1. The subject (Aesthetics) is very big and entirely misunderstood as far as I can see. The use of such a word as 'beautiful' is even more apt to be misunderstood if you look at the linguistic form of sentences in which it occurs than most other words. 'Beautiful' [and 'good'—R] is an adjective, so you are inclined to say: "This has a certain quality, that of being beautiful".

2. We are going from one subject-matter of philosophy to another, from one group of words to another group of words.

3. An intelligent way of dividing up a book on philosophy would be into parts of speech, kinds of words. Where in fact you would have to distinguish far more parts of speech than an ordinary grammar does. You would talk for hours and hours on the verbs 'seeing', 'feeling', etc., verbs describing personal experience. We get a peculiar kind of confusion or confusions which comes up with all these words.[1] You would have another chapter on numerals—here there would be another kind of confusion: a chapter on 'all', 'any', 'some', etc.—another kind of confusion: a chapter on 'you', 'I', etc.—another kind: a chapter on 'beautiful', 'good'—another kind. We get into a new group of confusions; language plays us entirely new tricks.

4. I have often compared language to a tool chest, containing a hammer, chisel, matches, nails, screws, glue. It is not a chance that all these things have been put together—but there are important differences between the different tools—they are used in a family of ways—though nothing could be more different than glue and a chisel. There is constant surprise at the new tricks language plays on us when we get into a new field.

5. One thing we always do when discussing a word is to ask how we were taught it. Doing this on the one hand destroys a variety of misconceptions, on the other hand gives you a primitive language in which the word is used. Although this language is not what you talk when you are twenty, you get a

[1] Here we find similarities—we find peculiar sorts of confusion which come up with *all* these words.—R.

rough approximation to what kind of language game is going to be played. Cf. How did we learn 'I dreamt so and so'? The interesting point is that we didn't learn it by being shown a dream. If you ask yourself how a child learns 'beautiful', 'fine', etc., you find it learns them roughly as interjections. ('Beautiful' is an odd word to talk about because it's hardly ever used.) A child generally applies a word like 'good' first to food. One thing that is immensely important in teaching is exaggerated gestures and facial expressions. The word is taught as a substitute for a facial expression or a gesture. The gestures, tones of voice, etc., in this case are expressions of approval. What *makes* the word an interjection of approval?[1] It is the game it appears in, not the form of words. (If I had to say what is the main mistake made by philosophers of the present generation, including Moore, I would say that it is that when language is looked at, what is looked at is a form of words and not the use made of the form of words.) Language is a characteristic part of a large group of activities—talking, writing, travelling on a bus, meeting a man, etc.[2] We are concentrating, not on the words 'good' or 'beautiful', which are entirely uncharacteristic, generally just subject and predicate ('This is beautiful'), but on the occasions on which they are said—on the enormously complicated situation in which the aesthetic expression has a place, in which the expression itself has almost a negligible place.

6. If you came to a foreign tribe, whose language you didn't know at all and you wished to know what words corresponded to 'good', 'fine', etc., what would you look for? You would look for smiles, gestures, food, toys. ([Reply to objection:] If you went to Mars and men were spheres with sticks coming out, you wouldn't know what to look for. Or if you went to a tribe where noises made with the mouth were just breathing or making music, and language was made with the ears. Cf. "When you see trees swaying about they are talking to one another." ("Every-

[1] And not of disapproval or of surprise, for example?
(The child understands the gestures which you use in teaching him. If he did not, he could understand nothing.)—R.

[2] When we build houses, we talk and write. When I take a bus, I say to the conductor: 'Threepenny.' We are concentrating not just on the word or the sentence in which it is used—which is highly uncharacteristic—but on the occasion on which it is said: the framework in which (nota bene) the actual aesthetic judgment is practically nothing at all.—R.

thing has a soul.") You compare the branches with arms. Certainly we must interpret the gestures of the tribe on the analogy of ours.) How far this takes us from normal aesthetics [and ethics—T]. We don't start from certain words, but from certain occasions or activities.

7. A characteristic thing about our language is that a large number of words used under these circumstances are adjectives —'fine', 'lovely', etc. But you see that this is by no means necessary. You saw that they were first used as interjections. Would it matter if instead of saying "This is lovely", I just said "Ah!" and smiled, or just rubbed my stomach? As far as these primitive languages go, problems about what these words are about, what their real subject is, [which is called 'beautiful' or 'good'.—R.][1] don't come up at all.

8. It is remarkable that in real life, when aesthetic judgements are made, aesthetic adjectives such as 'beautiful', 'fine', etc., play hardly any role at all. Are aesthetic adjectives used in a musical criticism? You say: "Look at this transition",[2] or [Rhees] "The passage here is incoherent". Or you say, in a poetical criticism, [Taylor]: "His use of images is precise". The words you use are more akin to 'right' and 'correct' (as these words are used in ordinary speech) than to 'beautiful' and 'lovely'.[3]

9. Words such as 'lovely' are first used as interjections. Later they are used on very few occasions. We might say of a piece of music that it is lovely, by this not praising it but giving it a character. (A lot of people, of course, who can't express themselves properly use the word very frequently. As they use it, it is used as an interjection.) I might ask: "For what melody would I most like to use the word 'lovely'?" I might choose between calling a melody 'lovely' and calling it 'youthful'. It is stupid to call a piece of music 'Spring Melody' or 'Spring Symphony'. But the word 'springy' wouldn't be absurd at all, any more than 'stately' or 'pompous'.

[1] What the thing that is really good is—T.

[2] 'The transition was made in the right way.'—T.

[3] It would be better to use 'lovely' descriptively, on a level with 'stately', 'pompous,' etc.—T.

10. If I were a good draughtsman, I could convey an innumerable number of expressions by four strokes—

Such words as 'pompous' and 'stately' could be expressed by faces. Doing this, our descriptions would be much more flexible and various than they are as expressed by adjectives. If I say of a piece of Schubert's that it is melancholy, that is like giving it a face (I don't express approval or disapproval). I could instead use gestures or [Rhees] dancing. In fact, if we want to be exact, we do use a gesture or a facial expression.

11. [*Rhees*: What rule are we using or referring to when we say: "This is the correct way"? If a music teacher says a piece *should* be played this way and plays it, what is he appealing to?]

12. Take the question: "How should poetry be read? What is the correct way of reading it?" If you are talking about blank verse the right way of reading it might be stressing it correctly—you discuss how far you should stress the rhythm and how far you should hide it. A man says it ought to be read *this* way and reads it out to you. You say: "Oh yes. Now it makes sense." There are cases of poetry which should almost be scanned—where the metre is as clear as crystal—others where the metre is entirely in the background. I had an experience with the 18th century poet Klopstock.[1] I found that the way to read him was to stress his metre abnormally. Klopstock put ⏑—⏑ (etc.) in front of his poems. When I read his poems in this new way, I said: "Ah-ha, now I know why he did this." What had happened? I had read this kind of stuff and had been moderately bored, but when I read it in this particular way, intensely, I smiled, said: "This is *grand*," etc. But I might not have said anything. The important fact was that I read it again and again. When I read these poems I made gestures and facial expressions which were what would be called gestures of approval. But the important

[1] Friedrich Gottlieb Klopstock (1724–1803). Wittgenstein is referring to the Odes. (*Gesammelte Werke*, Stuttgart, 1886–7). Klopstock believed that poetic diction was distinct from popular language. He rejected rhyme as vulgar and introduced instead the metres of ancient literature.—Ed.

thing was that I read the poems entirely differently, more intensely, and said to others: "Look! This is how they should be read."[1] Aesthetic adjectives played hardly any rôle.

13. What does a person who knows a good suit say when trying on a suit at the tailor's? "That's the right length", "That's too short", "That's too narrow". Words of approval play no rôle, although he will look pleased when the coat suits him. Instead of "That's too short" I might say "Look!" or instead of "Right" I might say "Leave it as it is". A good cutter may not use any words at all, but just make a chalk mark and later alter it. How do I show my approval of a suit? Chiefly by wearing it often, liking it when it is seen, etc.

14. (If I give you the light and shadow on a body in a picture I can thereby give you the shape of it. But if I give you the high-lights in a picture you don't know what the shape is.)

15. In the case of the word 'correct' you have a variety of related cases. There is first the case in which you learn the rules. The cutter learns how long a coat is to be, how wide the sleeve must be, etc. He learns rules—he is drilled—as in music you are drilled in harmony and counterpoint. Suppose I went in for tailoring and I first learnt all the rules, I might have, on the whole, two sorts of attitude. (1) Lewy says: "This is too short." I say: "No. It is right. It is according to the rules." (2) I develop a feeling for the rules. I interpret the rules. I might say: "No. It isn't right. It isn't according to the rules."[2] Here I would be making an aesthetic judgement about the thing which is according to the rules in sense (1). On the other hand, if I hadn't learnt the rules, I wouldn't be able to make the aesthetic judgement. In learning the rules you get a more and more refined judgement. Learning the rules actually changes your judgement. (Although, if you haven't learnt Harmony and haven't a good ear, you may nevertheless detect any disharmony in a sequence of chords.)

16. You could regard the rules laid down for the measurement of a coat as an expression of what certain people want.[3] People separated on the point of what a coat should measure:

[1] If we speak of the right way to read a piece of poetry—approval enters, but it plays a fairly small rôle in the situation.—R.

[2] 'Don't you see that if we made it broader, it isn't right and it isn't according to the rules.'—R.

[3] These may be extremely explicit and taught, or not formulated at all.—T.

there were some who didn't care if it was broad or narrow, etc.; there were others who cared an enormous lot.[1] The rules of harmony, you can say, expressed the way people wanted chords to follow—their wishes crystallized in these rules (the word 'wishes' is much too vague.)[2] All the greatest composers wrote in accordance with them. ([Reply to objection:] You can say that every composer changed the rules, but the variation was very slight; not all the rules were changed. The music was still good by a great many of the old rules.—This though shouldn't come in here.)

17. In what we call the Arts a person who has judgement developes. (A person who has a judgement doesn't mean a person who says 'Marvellous!' at certain things.)[3] If we talk of aesthetic judgements, we think, among a thousand things, of the Arts. When we make an aesthetic judgement about a thing, we do not just gape at it and say: "Oh! How marvellous!" We distinguish between a person who knows what he is talking about and a person who doesn't.[4] If a person is to admire English poetry, he must know English. Suppose that a Russian who doesn't know English is overwhelmed by a sonnet admitted to be good. We would say that he does not know what is in it at all. Similarly, of a person who doesn't know metres but who is overwhelmed, we would say that he doesn't know what's in it. In music this is more pronounced. Suppose there is a person who admires and enjoys what is admitted to be good but can't remember the simplest tunes, doesn't know when the bass comes in, etc. We say he hasn't seen what's in it. We use the phrase 'A man is musical' not so as to call a man musical if he says "Ah!" when a piece of music is played, any more than we call a dog musical if it wags its tail when music is played.[5]

[1] But—it is just a fact that people have laid down such and such rules. We say 'people' but in fact it was a particular class. . . . When we say 'people', these were *some* people.—R.

[2] And although we have talked of 'wishes' here, the fact is just that these rules were laid down.—R.

[3] In what we call the arts there developed what we call a 'judge'—i.e. one who has judgment. This does not mean just someone who admires or does not admire. We have an entirely new element.—R.

[4] He must react in a consistent way over a long period. Must know all sorts of things.—T.

[5] Cf. the person who likes hearing music but cannot talk about it at all, and is quite unintelligent on the subject. 'He is musical'. We do not say this if he is just happy when he hears music and the other things aren't present.—T.

18. The word we ought to talk about is 'appreciated'. What does appreciation consist in ?

19. If a man goes through an endless number of patterns in a tailor's, [and] says: "No. This is slightly too dark. This is slightly too loud", etc., he is what we call an appreciator of material. That he is an appreciator is not shown by the interjections he uses, but by the way he chooses, selects, etc. Similarly in music: "Does this harmonize? No. The bass is not quite loud enough. Here I just want something different. . . ." This is what we call an appreciation.

20. It is not only difficult to describe what appreciation consists in, but impossible. To describe what it consists in we would have to describe the whole environment.

21. I know exactly what happens when a person who knows a lot about suits goes to the tailor, also I know what happens when a person who knows nothing about suits goes—what he says, how he acts, etc.[1] There is an extraordinary number of different cases of appreciation. And, of course, what I know is nothing compared to what one could know. I would have—to say what appreciation is—e.g. to explain such an enormous wart as arts and crafts, such a particular kind of disease. Also I would have to explain what our photographers do today—and why it is impossible to get a decent picture of your friend even if you pay £1,000.

22. You can get a picture of what you may call a very high culture, e.g. German music in the last century and the century before, and what happens when this deteriorates. A picture of what happens in Architecture when you get imitations—or when thousands of people are interested in the minutest details. A picture of what happens when a dining-room table is chosen more or less at random, when no one knows where it came from.[2]

23. We talked of correctness. A good cutter won't use any words except words like 'Too long', 'All right'. When we talk of

[1] That is aesthetics.—T.

[2] Explain what happens when a craft deteriorates. A period in which everything is fixed and extraordinary care is lavished on certain details; and a period in which everything is copied and nothing is thought about.—T.

A great number of people are highly interested in a detail of a dining-room chair. And then there is a period when a dining-room chair is in the drawing-room and no one knows where this came from or that people had once given enormous thought in order to know how to design it.—R.

a Symphony of Beethoven we don't talk of correctness. Entirely different things enter. One wouldn't talk of appreciating the *tremendous* things in Art. In certain styles in Architecture a door is correct, and the thing is you appreciate it. But in the case of a Gothic Cathedral what we do is not at all to find it correct—it plays an entirely different rôle with us.[1] The entire *game* is different. It is as different as to judge a human being and on the one hand to say 'He behaves well' and on the other hand 'He made a great impression on me'.

24. 'Correctly', 'charmingly', 'finely', etc. play an entirely different rôle. Cf. the famous address of Buffon—a terrific man—on style in writing; making ever so many distinctions which I only understand vaguely but which he didn't mean vaguely—all kinds of nuances like 'grand', 'charming', 'nice'.[2]

25. The words we call expressions of aesthetic judgement play a very complicated rôle, but a very definite rôle, in what we call a culture of a period. To describe their use or to describe what you mean by a cultured taste, you have to describe a culture.[3] What we now call a cultured taste perhaps didn't exist in the Middle Ages. An entirely different game is played in different ages.

26. What belongs to a language game is a whole culture. In describing musical taste you have to describe whether children give concerts, whether women do or whether men only give them, etc., etc.[4] In aristocratic circles in Vienna people had [such and such] a taste, then it came into bourgeois circles and women joined choirs, etc. This is an example of tradition in music.

27. [*Rhees*: Is there tradition in Negro art? Could a European appreciate Negro art?]

28. What would tradition in Negro Art be? That women wear cut-grass skirts? etc., etc. I don't know. I don't know how Frank Dobson's appreciation of Negro Art compares with an

[1] Here there is no question of *degree*.—R.

[2] *Discours sur le style*: the address on his reception into L'Academie Française. 1753.—Ed.

[3] To describe a set of aesthetic rules fully means really to describe the culture of a period.—T.

[4] That children are taught by adults who go to concerts, etc., that the schools are like they are, etc.—R.

educated Negro's.[1] If you say he appreciates it, I don't yet know what this means.[2] He may fill his room with objects of Negro Art. Does he just say: "Ah!"? Or does he do what the best-Negro musicians do? Or does he agree or disagree with so and so about it? You may call this appreciation. Entirely different to an educated Negro's. Though an educated Negro may also have Negro objects of art in his room. The Negro's and Frank Dobson's are different appreciations altogether. You do something different with them. Suppose Negroes dress in their own way and I say I appreciate a good Negro tunic—does this mean I would have one made, or that I would say (as at the tailor's): "No... this is too long", or does it mean I say: "How charming!"?

29. Suppose Lewy has what is called a cultured taste in painting. This is something entirely different to what was called a cultured taste in the fifteenth century. An entirely different game was played. He does something entirely different with it to what a man did then.

30. There are lots of people, well-offish, who have been to good schools, who can afford to travel about and see the Louvre, etc., and who know a lot about and can talk fluently about dozens of painters. There is another person who has seen very few paintings, but who looks intensely at one or two paintings which make a profound impression on him.[3] Another person who is broad, neither deep nor wide. Another person who is very narrow, concentrated and circumscribed. Are these different kinds of appreciation? They may all be called 'appreciation'.

31. You talk in entirely different terms of the Coronation robe of Edward II and of a dress suit.[4] What did *they* do and say about Coronation robes? Was the Coronation robe made by a tailor? Perhaps it was designed by Italian artists who had their own traditions; never seen by Edward II until he put it on. Questions like 'What standards were there?', etc. are all relevant

[1] Frank Dobson (1888–1963) painter and sculptor; was the first to bring to England the interest in African and Asian sculpture which characterized the work of Picasso and the other Cubists during the years immediately preceeding and following the First World War.—Ed.

[2] Here you haven't made what you mean by 'appreciate Negro Art' clear.—T.

[3] Someone who has not travelled but who makes certain observations which show that he 'really does appreciate' . . . an appreciation which concentrates on one thing and is very deep—so that you would give your last penny for it.—R.

[4] Edward the Confessor.—T.

to the question 'Could you criticize the robe as they critized it?'. You appreciate it in an entirely different way; your attitude to it is entirely different to that of a person living at the time it was designed. On the other hand 'This is a fine Coronation robe!' might have been said by a man at the time in exactly the same way as a man says it now.

32. I draw your attention to differences and say: "Look how different these differences are!" "Look what is in common to the different cases", "Look what is common to Aesthetic judgements". An immensely complicated family of cases is left, with the highlight—the expression of admiration, a smile or a gesture, etc.

33. [Rhees asked Wittgenstein some question about his 'theory' of deterioration.]

Do you think I have a theory? Do you think I'm saying what deterioration is? What I do is describe different things called deterioration. I might approve deterioration—"All very well your fine musical culture; I'm very glad children don't learn harmony now." [*Rhees*: Doesn't what you say imply a preference for using 'deterioration' in certain ways?] All right, if you like, but this by the way—no, it is no matter. My example of deterioration is an example of something I know, perhaps something I dislike—I don't know. 'Deterioration' applies to a tiny bit I may know.

34. Our dress is in a way simpler than dress in the 18th century and more a dress adapted to certain violent activities, such as bicycling, walking, etc. Suppose we notice a similar change in Architecture and in hairdressing, etc. Suppose I talked of the deterioration of the style of living.[1] If someone asks: "What do you mean by deterioration?" I describe, give examples. You use 'deterioration' on the one hand to describe a particular kind of development, on the other hand to express disapproval. I may join it up with the things I like; you with the things you dislike. But the word may be used without any affective element; you use it to describe a particular kind of thing that happened.[2] It was more like using a technical term—possibly,

[1] Deterioration of style and of living.—R.

[2] 'Deterioration' gets its sense from the examples I can give. 'That's a deterioration,' may be an expression of disapproval or a description.

though not at all necessarily, with a derogatory element in it. You may say in protest, when I talk of deterioration: "But this was very good." I say: "All right. But this wasn't what I was talking about. I used it to describe a particular kind of development."

35. In order to get clear about aesthetic words you have to describe ways of living.[1] We think we have to talk about aesthetic judgements like 'This is beautiful', but we find that if we have to talk about aesthetic judgements we don't find these words at all, but a word used something like a gesture, accompanying a complicated activity.[2]

36. [*Lewy*: If my landlady says a picture is lovely and I say it is hideous, we don't contradict one another.]

In a sense [and in *certain examples*—R] you do contradict one another. She dusts it carefully, looks at it often, etc. You want to throw it in the fire. This is just the stupid kind of example which is given in philosophy, as if things like 'This is hideous', 'This is lovely' were the only kinds of things ever said. But it is only one thing amongst a vast realm of other things—one special case. Suppose the landlady says: "This is hideous", and you say: "This is lovely"—all right, that's that.

II

1. One interesting thing is the idea that people have of a kind of science of Aesthetics. I would almost like to talk of what could be meant by Aesthetics.

2. You might think Aesthetics is a science telling us what's beautiful—almost too ridiculous for words. I suppose it ought to include also what sort of coffee tastes well.[3]

3. I see roughly this—there is a realm of utterance of delight, when you taste pleasant food or smell a pleasant smell, etc., then there is the realm of Art which is quite different, though often you

[1] Cf. 'This is a fine dress.'—R.

[2] The judgment is a gesture accompanying a vast structure of actions not expressed by one judgment.—R.

'This is fine' is on a level with a gesture, almost—connected with all sorts of other gestures and actions and a whole situation and a culture. In Aesthetics just as in the arts what we called expletives play a very small part. The adjectives used in these are closer related to 'correct'.—T.

[3] It is hard to find boundaries.—R.

may make the same face when you hear a piece of music as when you taste good food. (Though you may cry at something you like very much.)

4. Supposing you meet someone in the street and he tells you he has lost his greatest friend, in a voice extremely expressive of his emotion.[1] You might say: "It was extraordinarily beautiful, the way he expressed himself." Supposing you then asked: "What similarity has my admiring this person with my eating vanilla ice and liking it?" To compare them seems almost disgusting. (But you can connect them by intermediate cases.) Suppose someone said: "But this is a quite different kind of delight." But did you learn two meanings of 'delight'? You use the same word on both occasions.[2] There is some connection between these delights. Although in the first case the emotion of delight would in our judgement hardly count.[3]

5. It is like saying: "I classify works of Art in this way: at some I look up and at some I look down." This way of classifying might be interesting.[4] We might discover all sorts of connections between looking up or down at works of Art and looking up or down at other things. If we found, perhaps, that eating vanilla ice made us look up, we might not attach great importance to looking up. There may be a realm, a small realm of experiences which may make me look up or down where I can infer a lot from the fact that I looked up or down; another realm of experiences where nothing can be inferred from my looking up or down.[5] Cf wearing blue or green trousers may in a certain society mean a lot, but in another society it may not mean anything.

6. What are expressions of liking something? Is it only what we say or interjections we use or faces we make? Obviously not. It is, often, how often I read something or how often I wear a suit. Perhaps I won't even say: "It's fine", but wear it often and look at it.[6]

[1] Someone . . . who tells you he has lost his friend, in a restrained way.—R.

[2] But notice that you use the same word and not in the same chance way yon use the same word 'bank' for two things [like 'river bank' and 'money bank'—R.] —T.

[3] Although in the first case the gesture or expression of delight may be most unimportant in a way.—T.

[4] You might discover further characters of things which make us look up—.R.

[5] Some one might exaggerate the importance of the type of indication.—T.

[6] If I like a suit I may buy it, or wear it often—without interjections or making faces.—R. I may never smile at it.—T.

7. Suppose we build houses and we give doors and windows certain dimensions. Does the fact that we *like* these dimensions necessarily show in anything we say? Is what we like necessarily shown by an expression of *liking*?[1] [For instance—R] suppose our children draw windows and when they draw them in the wrong way we punish them. Or when someone builds a certain house we refuse to live in it or run away.

8. Take the case of fashions. How does a fashion come about? Say, we wear lapels broader than last year. Does this mean that the tailors like them better broader? No, not necessarily. He cuts it like this and this year he makes it broader. Perhaps this year he finds it too narrow and makes it wider. Perhaps no expression [of delight—R] is used at all.[2]

9. You design a door and look at it and say: "Higher, higher, higher . . . oh, all right."[3] (Gesture) What is this? Is it an expression of content?

10. Perhaps the most important thing in connection with aesthetics is what may be called aesthetic reactions, e.g. discontent, disgust, discomfort. The expression of discontent is not the same as the expression of discomfort. The expression of discontent says: "Make it higher . . . too low! . . . do something to this."

11. Is what I call an expression of discontent something like an expression of discomfort *plus* knowing the cause of the discomfort and asking for it to be removed? If I say: "This door is too low. Make it higher", should we say I know the cause of my discomfort?

12. 'Cause' is used in very many different ways, e.g.

(1) "What is the cause of unemployment?" "What is the cause of this expression?"

(2) "What was the cause of your jumping?" "That noise."

(3) "What was the cause of that wheel going round?" You trace a mechanism.[4]

[1] Our preferring these shows itself in all sorts of ways.—T.

[2] But the tailor does not say: 'This is nice.' He is a good cutter. He is just contented.—R. If you mean 'this year he cuts it broader' then you can say this. This way we are contented, the other not.—T.

[3] '. . . *there*: thank God.'—R. '. . . yes, that's right.'—T.

[4] Cause: (1) Experiment and statistics.
(2) Reason.
(3) Mechanism.—T.

13. [*Redpath*: "Making the door higher removes your discontent."]

Wittgenstein asked: "Why is this a bad way of putting it?" It is in the wrong form because it presupposes '—removes—'.

14. Saying you know the cause of your discomfort could mean two things.

(1) I predict correctly that if you lower the door, I will be satisfied.

(2) But that when in fact I say: "Too high!" 'Too high!' is in this case not conjecture. Is 'Too high' comparable with 'I think I had too many tomatoes today'?

15. If I ask: "If I make it lower will your discomfort cease?", you may say: "I'm *sure* it will." The important thing is that I say: "Too high!" It is a reaction analogous to my taking my hand away from a hot plate—which may not relieve my discomfort. The reaction peculiar to this discomfort is saying 'Too high' or whatever it is.

16. To say: "I feel discomfort and know the cause", is entirely misleading because 'know the cause' normally means something quite different. How misleading it is depends on whether when you said: "I know the cause", you meant it to be an explanation or not. 'I feel discomfort and know the cause' makes it sound as if there were two things going on in my soul—discomfort and knowing the cause.

17. In these cases the word 'cause' is hardly ever used at all. You use 'why?' and 'because', but not 'cause'.[1]

18. We have here a kind of discomfort which you may call 'directed', e.g. if I am afraid of you, my discomfort is directed.[2] Saying 'I know the cause' brings in mind the case of statistics or tracing a mechanism. If I say: "I know the cause", it looks as if I had analysed the feelings (as I analyse the feeling of hearing my own voice and, at the same time, rubbing my hands) which, of course, I haven't done. We have given, as it were, a *grammatical* explanation [in saying, the feeling is 'directed'].

19. There is a 'Why?' to aesthetic discomfort not a 'cause' to it. The expression of discomfort takes the form of a criticism

[1] Why are you disgusted? Because it is too high.—R.

[2] What is the advantage of 'My feeling of fear is directed' as opposed to 'I know the cause'?—R.

and not 'My mind is not at rest' or something. It might take the form of looking at a picture and saying: "What's wrong with it?"[1]

20. It's all very well to say: "Can't we get rid of this analogy?" Well, we cannot. If we think of discomfort—cause, pain—cause of pain naturally suggests itself.

21. The cause, in the sense of the object it is directed to is also the cause in other senses. When you remove it, the discomfort ceases and what not.

22. If one says: "Can we be immediately aware of the cause?", the first thing that comes into our mind is not statistics [(as in 'the cause of the rise in unemployment')—R], but tracing a mechanism. It has so very often been said that if something has been caused by something else this is only a matter of concomitance. Isn't this very queer? Very queer. 'It's only concomitance' shows you think it can be something else.[2] It could be an experiential proposition, but then I don't know what it would be. Saying this shows you know of something different, i.e. connection. What are they denying when they say: "There is no necessary connection"?

23. You say constantly in philosophy things like: "People say there is a super-mechanism, but there isn't." But no one knows what a super-mechanism is.

24. (The idea of a super-mechanism doesn't really come in here. What comes in is the idea of a mechanism.)

25. We have the idea of a super-mechanism when we talk of logical necessity, e.g. physics tried as an ideal to reduce things to mechanisms or something hitting something else.[3]

26. We say that people condemn a man to death and then we say the Law condemns him to death. "Although the Jury can

[1] If I look at a picture and say: 'What's wrong with this?', then it is better to say that my feeling has direction, and not that my feeling has a cause and I don't know what it is. Otherwise we suggest an analogy with 'pain' and 'cause of pain'—i.e. what you have eaten. This is wrong or misleading, because, although we do use the word 'cause' in the sense of 'what it is directed to' ('What made you jump?'—'Seeing him appear in the doorway'), we often use it in other senses also.—R.

[2] If you say: 'To speak of the cause of some development is only to speak of the concomitants'—'cause is only a question of concomitants'—then if you put 'only', you are admitting that it *could* be something else. It means that you know of something entirely different.—R.

[3] You want to say: 'Surely there is a connection.' But what is a connection? Well, levers, chains, cogwheels. These are connections, and here we have them. but here what we ought to explain is 'super'.—R.

pardon [acquit?] him, the Law can't." (This *may* mean the Law can't take bribes, etc.) The idea of something super-strict, something stricter than any Judge can be,[1] super-rigidity. The point being, you are inclined to ask: "Do we have a picture of something more rigorous?" Hardly. But we are inclined to express ourselves in the form of a superlative.

27.

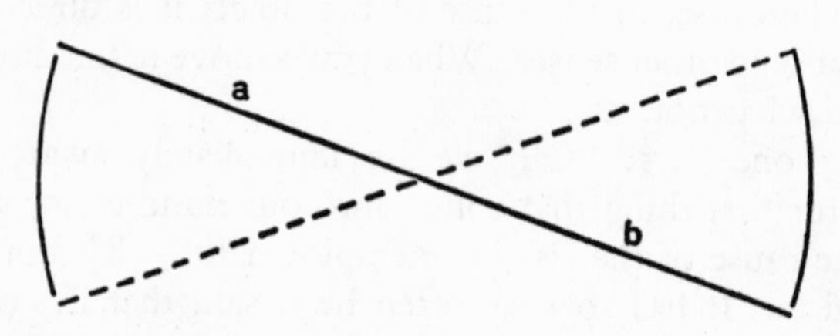

Cf. a lever-fulcrum. The idea of a super-hardness. "The geometrical lever is harder than any lever can be. It can't bend." Here you have the case of logical necessity. "Logic is a mechanism made of an infinitely hard material. Logic cannot bend.'[2] (Well, no more it can.) This is the way we arrive at a super-something. This is the way certain superlatives come about, how they are used, e.g. the infinite.

28. People would say that even in the case of tracing a mechanism there is also concomitance. But need there be? I just follow the string to the person at the other end.

29. Suppose there was a super-mechanism in the sense that there was a mechanism inside the string. Even if there was such a mechanism, it would do no good. You do recognize tracing the mechanism as tracing a peculiar kind of causal reaction.

30. You wish to get rid of the idea of connection altogether. "This is also only concomitance." Then there is nothing more to be said.[3] You would have to specify what is a case you wouldn't

[1] Something that cannot be swayed.—R.

[2] Suppose that we treat of kinematics. Give the distance of the lever from the point, and calculate the distance of the arc.

But then we say: 'If the lever is made of metal, however hard, it will bend a little, and the point will not come just there.' And so we have the idea of a super-rigidity: the idea of a *geometrical* lever which *cannot* bend. Here we have the idea of logical necessity: a mechanism of infinitely hard material.—R.

If someone says: 'You mustn't think that logic is made of an infinitely hard material', you must ask: 'What mustn't I think?'—T.

[3] What we call '*explanation*' is a form of *connection*. And we wish to get rid of connection altogether. We wish to get rid of the notion of mechanism, and say: 'It's all concomitants.' Why 'all'?—R.

call concomitance. "Tracing a mechanism is only finding concomitance. In the end it can all be reduced to concomitance." It It might be proved that people never traced a mechanism unless they had had a lot of experience of a certain sort. This could be put in the way: "It all reduces to concomitance."

31. Cf. "Physics doesn't explain anything. It just describes cases of concomitance."

32. You could mean by 'There is no super-mechanism', 'Don't imagine mechanisms between the atoms in the case of a lever. There aren't any mechanisms there'.[1] (You are taking for granted the atomistic picture.[2] What does this come to? We are so used to this picture that it's as though we had all seen atoms. Every educated eight-year old child knows that things are made of atoms. We would think it lack of education if a person didn't think of a rod as being made of atoms.)

33. (You can look on the mechanism as a set of concomitant causal phenomena. You don't, of course.) You say: "Well, this moves this, this this, this this, and so on."

34. Tracing a mechanism is one way of finding the cause; we speak of 'the cause' in this case. But if cases of wheels made of butter and looking like steel were frequent we might say: "This ('this wheel') is not the only cause at all. This may only look like a mechanism."[3]

35. People often say that aesthetics is a branch of psychology. The idea is that once we are more advanced, everything—all the mysteries of Art—will be understood by psychological experiments. Exceedingly stupid as the idea is, this is roughly it.

36. Aesthetic questions have nothing to do with psychological experiments, but are answered in an entirely different way.[4]

[1] You reduce the actual mechanism to a more complicated atomic mechanism, but don't go on.—T.

[2] We might have a primitive mechanism. Then we have the picture of its all being formed of particles—atoms, etc. And we might then want to say: 'Don't go on to think of atoms between these atoms.' Here we take for granted the atomic picture—which is a queer business. If we had to say what a super-mechanism was, we might say it was one which did not consist of atoms: bits of the mechanism were just solid.—R.

[3] We are constantly inclined to reduce things to other things. So excited by finding that it's sometimes concomitance, we wish to say it's all *really* concomitance. —T.

[4] I wish to make it clear that the important problems in aesthetics are not settled by psychological research.—T.

These problems are answered in a different way—more in the form 'What is in my mind when I say so and so?'—R.

37. "What is in my mind when I say so and so?"[1] I write a sentence. One word isn't the one I need. I find the right word. "What is it I want to say? Oh yes, that is what I wanted." The answer in these cases is the one that satisfied you, e.g. someone says (as we often say in philosophy): "I will tell you what is at the back of your mind: . . ."

"Oh yes, quite so."

The criterion for it being the one that was in your mind is that when I tell you, you agree. This is not what is called a psychological experiment. An example of a psychological experiment is: you have twelve subjects, put same question to each and the result is that each says such and such, i.e. the result is something statistical.[2]

38. You could say: "An aesthetic explanation is not a causal explanation."[3]

39. Cf. Freud: *Wit and the Unconscious*. Freud wrote about jokes. You might call the explanation Freud gives a causal explanation. "If it is not causal, how do you know it's correct?" You say: "Yes, that's right."[4] Freud transforms the joke into a different form which is recognized by us as an expression of the chain of ideas which led us from one end to another of a joke. An entirely new account of a correct explanation. Not one agreeing with experience, but one accepted. You have to give the explanation that is accepted. This is the whole point of the explanation.

40. Cf. "Why do I say "Higher!"?" with "Why do I say "I have a pain"?"[5]

[1] Compare: 'What people really want to say is so and so.'—R.

[2] Is this a narrowing of the sense of psychological experiment?—T.

[3] It is true that 'psychology' is used in very different ways. We could say that aesthetic explanation is not causal explanation. Or that it is causal explanation of this sort: that the person who agrees with you sees the cause at once.—R.

[4] All we can say is that if it is presented to you, you say 'Yes, that's what happened.'—R.

[5] The unrest when you ask: 'Why?' in this sort of case is similar to the unrest in the case of 'Why?' when you look for the mechanism. 'Explanation' here is on the level of utterance. In some respect on a level. Cf. the two games with 'He's in pain.' Cf the two games with 'He's in pain.'—T.

Here 'explanation' is on the same level as an utterance—where the utterance (when you say that you have pain, for instance) is the sole criterion. Explanation here is like an utterance supplied by another person—like teaching him to cry. (This takes the surprisingness away from the fact that the whole point of an explanation is that it is accepted. There are corresponding to these explanations utterances which look like this; just as there are utterances which look like assertions.)—R.

III

1. One asks such a question as 'What does this remind me of?" or one says of a piece of music: "This is like some sentence, but what sentence is it like?"[1] Various things are suggested; one thing, as you say, clicks. What does it mean, it 'clicks'? Does it do anything you can compare to the noise of a click? Is there the ringing of a bell, or something comparable?[2]

2. It is as though you needed some criterion, namely the clicking, to know the right thing has happened.[3]

3. The comparison is, that some one particular phenomenon happened other than my saying: "That's right." You say: "That explanation is the right one which clicks." Suppose someone said: "The tempo of that song will be all right when I can hear distinctly such and such."[4] I have pointed to a phenomenon which, if it is the case, will make me satisfied.

4. You might say the clicking is that I'm satisfied. Take a pointer moving into place opposite another one. You are satisfied *when* the two pointers are opposite one another.[5] And you could have said this in advance.[6]

5. We are again and again using this simile of something clicking or fitting, when really there is nothing that clicks or that fits anything.

6. I should like to talk of the sort of explanation one longs for when one talks about an aesthetic impression.

7. People still have the idea that psychology is one day going to explain all our aesthetic judgements, and they mean experimental psychology. This is very funny—very funny indeed. There doesn't seem any connection between what psychologists do and any judgement about a work of art. We

[1] There may be an 'explanation' in the form of an answer to a question like 'What does this remind me of?'. In a piece of music there may be a theme of which I say. . .—R.

[2] Does it click in any sense? So that, for instance, you say: 'Now it has made that noise'? Of course not. What do we compare the clicking with here? 'With a feeling,' 'So you have a feeling?' Do you have a sign that it has fallen into place? —R.

[3] Is there any necessary criterion for this happening?—T.

[4] If it is sung slowly. . .—R. played by degrees faster. . .—T.

[5] (Something moving along a circumference, clicks when it falls into place.) —T.

[6] But why not say the clicking is just that I am satisfied? Whereas it might look as though clicking were something else, which I wait for, and when it comes I am satisfied. In some circumstances you *could* point to such a phenomenon.—R.

might examine what sort of thing we would call an explanation of an aesthetic judgement.

8. Supposing it was found that all our judgements proceeded from our brain. We discovered particular kinds of mechanism in the brain, formulated general laws, etc. One could show that this sequence of notes produces this particular kind of reaction; makes a man smile and say: "Oh, how wonderful."[1] (Mechanism for English language, etc.)[2] Suppose this were done, it might enable us to predict what a particular person would like and dislike. We could calculate these things. The question is whether this is the sort of explanation we should like to have when we are puzzled about aesthetic impressions, e.g. there is a puzzle—"Why do these bars give me such a peculiar impression?" Obviously it isn't this, i.e. a calculation, an account of reactions, etc., we want—apart from the obvious impossibility of the thing.

9. As far as one can see the puzzlement I am talking about can be cured only by peculiar kinds of comparisons, e.g. by an arrangement of certain musical figures, comparing their effect on us.[3] "If we put in this chord it does not have that effect; if we put in this chord it does." You could have a sentence and say "This sentence sounds queer somehow". You could point what's queer. What would be the criterion that you had pointed out the right thing? Suppose a poem sounded old-fashioned, what would be the criterion that you had found out what was old-fashioned in it. One criterion would be that when something was pointed out you were satisfied. And another criterion: "No-one would use that word today"[4]; here you might refer to a dictionary, ask other people, etc.[5] I *could* point out the wrong thing and yet you would still be satisfied.

10. Suppose someone heard syncopated music of Brahms played and asked: "What is the queer rhythm which makes me wobble?"[6] "It is the 3 against 4." One could play certain phrases

[1] If you knew the mechanism of molecules there, and then knew the sequence of notes in the music, we could show that. . .—R.

[2] That he says it in English and not in French would also be explained by the fact that something is embodied in his brain: we could see the differences.—R.

[3] When the written notes or the played notes are spread out, then you say. . .T.

[4] 'It is this word, you see. No one today would say so and so.'—R.

[5] Suppose you asked: 'What is it that sounds American about this sentence?' But you could find out whether the word was an americanism or not, for instance; other people might corroborate this.—R.

[6] Feel wobbly.—R.

and he would say: "Yes. It's this peculiar rhythm I meant." On the other hand, if he didn't agree, this wouldn't be the explanation.

11. The sort of explanation one is looking for when one is puzzled by an aesthetic impression is not a causal explanation, not one corroborated by experience or by statistics as to how people react.[1] One of the curious [characteristic—R] things about psychological experiments is that they have to be made on a number of subjects. It is the agreements of Smith, Jones and Robinson which allows you to give an explanation—in this sense of explanation, e.g. you can try out a piece of music in a psychological laboratory and get the result that the music acts in such and such a way under such and such a drug.[2] This is not what one means or what one is driving at by an investigation into aesthetics.

12. This is connected with the difference between cause and motive. In a law-court you are asked the motive of your action and you are supposed to know it. Unless you lie you are supposed to be able to tell the motive of your action. You are not supposed to know the laws by which your body and mind are governed. Why do they suppose you know it? Because you've had such a lot of experience with yourself? People sometimes say: "No-one can see inside you, but you can see inside yourself", as though being so near yourself, being yourself, you know your own mechanism.[3] But is it like that? "Surely he must know why he did it or why he said such and such."

13. One case is, where you give the reason for your doing something.[4] "Why did you write 6249 under the line?" You give the multiplication you had done. "I arrived at it by this multiplication." This is comparable to giving a mechanism. One might call it giving a motive for writing down the numbers. It means, I passed through such and such a process of reasoning.[5]

[1] You cannot arrive at the explanation by means of psychological experiment.—R.

[2] Or on people of a certain race.—R.

[3] Obviously this has nothing to do with your having observed yourself so often. (Often we do seem to suggest that because you are so near to yourself, you could see what happened. This is like knowing your own mechanism.)—R.

[4] There is one thing here that could be compared with knowing a mechanism—'Surely he must know why he did it, or why he said so and so.' But how do you know why you did it? There is one kind of case where the answer is to give the *reason*: you are writing out a multiplication, and I ask. . .—R.

[5] Where I give a reason in this sense. . .—R.

Here 'Why did you do it?' means 'How did you get there?'. You give a reason, the road you went.

14. If he tells us a peculiar process by which he arrived at the thing, this inclines us to say: "Only he knows the process which led to it."

15. Giving a reason sometimes means 'I actually went this way', sometimes 'I could have gone this way', i.e. sometimes what we say acts as a justification, not as a report of what was done, e.g. I *remember* the answer to a question; when asked why I give this answer, I gave a process leading to it, though I didn't go through this process.[1]

16. "Why did you do it?" Answer: "I said to myself such and such . . ." In many cases the motive is just what we give on being asked.[2]

17. When you ask: "Why did you do it?", in an enormous number of cases people give an answer—apodictic—and are unshakable about it, and in an enormous number of cases we accept the answer given. There are other cases where people say they have forgotten their motive. Other cases where you are puzzled immediately after you have done something and ask: "Why did I do this?"[3] Suppose Taylor was in this state and I said: "Look here, Taylor. The molecules in the sofa attract the molecules in your brain, etc. . . and so . . ."

18. Suppose Taylor and I are walking along the river and Taylor stretches out his hand and pushes me in the river. When I ask why he did this he says: "I was pointing out something to you", whereas the psycho-analyst says that Taylor subconsciously hated me.[4] Suppose e.g. it often happened that when two people were walking along a river:

(1) they were talking amicably;

[1] We may give the process which led to it before. Or it may be what we now see would justify it.—R.

(It is not a natural usage of 'motive'.) You might say: 'He knows what he was doing, nobody else does.'—T.

[2] Thus 'reason' does not always mean the same thing. And similarly with 'motive'. 'Why did you do it?' One sometimes answers: 'Well, I said to myself: "I must see him because he is ill." '—actually remembering having said things to oneself. Or again, in many cases the motive is the justification we give on being asked—just that.—R.

[3] But is it clear why one should be puzzled?—R.

[4] A lot of things confirm this. At the same time a psycho-analyst has another explanation.—T. We might have evidence that the psycho-analyst's explanation is correct.—R.

(2) one was obviously pointing out something and pushed the other in the river;

(3) the person pushed in had a similarity with the father of the other person.

Here we have two explanations:

(1) He subconsciously hated the other man.

(2) He was pointing at something.

19. Both explanations may be correct. When would we say that Taylor's explanation was correct? When he had never shown any unfriendly feelings, when a church-steeple and I were in his field of vision, and Taylor was known to be truthful. But, under the same circumstances, the psycho-analyst's explanation may also be correct.[1] Here there are two motives—conscious and unconscious. The games played with the two motives are utterly different.[2] The explanations could in a sense be contradictory and yet both be correct. (Love and Hate.)[3]

20. This connects up with something that Freud does. Freud does something which seems to me immensely wrong. He gives what he calls an interpretation of dreams. In his book *The Interpretation of Dreams* he describes one dream which he calls a 'beautiful dream' ['Ein schöner Traum'—R].[4] A patient, after saying that she had had a beautiful dream, described a dream in which she descended from a height, saw flowers and shrubs, broke off the branch of a tree, etc. Freud shows what he calls the 'meaning' of the dream. The coarsest sexual stuff, bawdy of the worst kind—if you wish to call it that—bawdy from A to Z. We know what we mean by bawdy. A remark sounds to the uninitiated harmless, but the initiated, say, chuckle when they hear it. Freud says the dream is bawdy. *Is* it bawdy? He shows relations between the dream images and certain objects of a sexual nature. The relation he establishes is roughly this. By a chain of associations which comes naturally under certain circumstances, this

[1] He hated me because I reminded him of something. And the psychoanalyst's statement is then corroborated. *How* corroborated?—R.

[2] Utterly different things are done with the statement of conscious motive and with the statement of unconscious motive.—R.

[3] One could be love and one could be hatred.—R.

[4] Freud's 'Ein schöner Traum' (*Die Traumdeutung* Frankfurt: Fisher Bücherei, 1961, p. 240) does not contain the features of the 'beautiful dream' described here. But the dream which does contain them (the 'flowery dream'—'Blumentraum'—p. 289) is in fact described as 'beautiful' or 'pretty' ('schöne'): 'Der schöne Traum wollte der Träumerin nach der Deutung gar nicht mehr gefallen.'—Ed.

leads to that, etc.[1] Does this prove that the dream is what is called bawdy? Obviously not. If a person talks bawdy he doesn't say something which seems to him harmless, and is then psycho-analysed.[2] Freud called this dream 'beautiful', putting 'beautiful' in inverted commas. But *wasn't* the dream beautiful? I would say to the patient: "Do these associations make the dream not beautiful? It was beautiful.[3] Why shouldn't it be?" I would say Freud had cheated the patient. Cf. scents made of things having intolerable smells. Could we therefore say: "The 'best' scent is really all sulphuric acid?"[4] Why did Freud give this explanation at all? Two things people might say:

(1) He wishes to explain everything nice in a nasty way, meaning almost that he is fond of bawdy. This is obviously not the case.

(2) The connections he makes interest people immensely. They have a charm. It is charming[5] to destroy prejudice.

21. Cf. "If we boil Redpath at 200° C. all that is left when the water vapour is gone is some ashes, etc.[6] This is all Redpath really is." Saying this might have a certain charm, but would be misleading to say the least.

22. The attraction of certain kinds of explanation is overwhelming. At a given time the attraction of a certain kind of explanation is greater than you can conceive.[7] In particular, explanation of the kind 'This is really only this'.

23. There is a strong tendency to say: "We can't get round the fact that this dream is really such and such."[8] It may be the fact that the explanation is extremely repellant that drives you to adopt it.

24. If someone says: "Why do you say it is really this? Obviously it is not this at all", it is in fact even difficult to see it as something else.

[1] From a flower to this, a tree to that, etc.—R.
[2] You dont say a person talks bawdy when his intention is innocent.—T.
[3] This is what is called beautiful.—T.
[4] If there is a connection between butyric acid which stinks and the best perfumes, could we on that account put 'the best perfume' in quotes.—T.
[5] To some people.—R.
[6] 'If we heat this man to 200 degrees Centegrade, the water evaporates . . .'—R.
[7] If you haven't just the right examples in mind.—T.
[8] If we see the connection of something like this beautiful dream to something ugly . . .—R.

25. Here is an extremely interesting psychological phenomenon, that this ugly explanation makes you say you really had these thoughts, whereas in any ordinary sense you really didn't.

(1) There is the process ['freier Einfall'—R] which connects certain parts of the dream with certain objects.

(2) There is the process 'So this is what I meant'. There is a maze for people to go astray in here.[1]

26. Suppose you were analysed when you had a stammer. (1) You may say that that explanation [analysis—R] is correct which cures the stammer. (2) If the stammer is not cured the criterion may be the person analysed saying: "This explanation is correct",[2] or agreeing that the explanation given him is correct. (3) Another criterion is that according to certain rules of experience[3] the explanation given is the correct one, whether the person to whom it is given adopts it or not.[4] Many of these explanations are adopted because they have a peculiar charm. The picture of people having subconscious thoughts has a charm. The idea of an underworld, a secret cellar. Something hidden, uncanny. Cf. Keller's two children putting a live fly in the head of a doll, burying the doll and then running away.[5] (Why do we do this sort of thing? This is the sort of thing we do do.) A lot of things one is ready to believe because they are uncanny.

27. One of the most important things about an explanation [in Physics R, T] is that it should work, that it should enable us to predict something [successfully—T]. Physics is connected with Engineering. The bridge must not fall down.

28. Freud says: "There are several instances (cf. Law) in the mind."[6] Many of these explanations (i.e. of psycho-analysis) are not borne out by experience, as an explanation in Physics is.[7] The

[1] These two need not go together. Either might work and the other not.—R.

[2] 'Oh yes, that's what I meant.'—R. Or you may say that the analogy is correct which the person analyzed agrees to.—T.

[3] Of explaining such phenomena.—R.

[4] Or you may say that the correct analogy is the accepted one. The one ordinarily given.—T.

[5] Gottfried Keller (1819–1890). A Swiss poet, novelist and short-story writer. The incident to which Wittgenstein refers occurs in *Romeo und Julia auf dem Dorfe*, *Werke V-VI*, Berlin, 1889, p. 84.—Ed.

[6] If you look at what Freud says in explanation—not in his clinical procedure, but, for instance, what we say about the different 'Instanzen' ('instances', in the sense in which we speak of a court of higher instance) of the mind.—R.

[7] An explanation in a different sense often. Its attractiveness is important, more important than in the case of an explanation in physics.—T.

attitude they express is important. They give us a picture which has a peculiar attraction for us.[1]

29. Freud has very intelligent reasons for saying what he says, great imagination and colossal prejudice, and prejudice which is very likely to mislead people.[2]

30. Suppose someone like Freud stresses enormously the importance of sexual motives:

(1) Sexual motives are immensely important.

(2) Often people have good reason to hide a sexual motive as a motive.[3]

31. Isn't this also a good reason for *admitting* sex as a motive for everything, for saying: "This is really at the bottom of everything"? Isn't it clear that a particular way of explaining can bring you to admit another thing. Suppose I show Redpath fifty cases where he admits a certain motive, twenty cases where this motive is an important link. I could make him admit it as a motive in all cases.[4]

32. Cf. The Darwin upheaval. One circle of admirers who said: "Of course", and another circle [of enemies—R] who said: "Of course not".[5] Why in the Hell should a man say 'of course'? (The idea was that of monocellular organisms becoming more and more complicated until they became mammals, men, etc.) Did anyone see this process happening? No. Has anyone seen it happening now? No. The evidence of breeding is just a drop in the bucket. But there were thousands of books in which this was said to be *the* obvious solution. People were *certain* on grounds which were extremely thin. Couldn't there have been an attitude which said: "I don't know. It is an interesting hypothesis which may eventually be well confirmed"?[6] This shows how you can be persuaded of a certain thing. In the end you

[1] This does not help us to *predict* anything, but it has a peculiar attraction.—R.

[2] People can be convinced of many things according to what you tell them.—R.

[3] It is disagreeable to have to admit it so often.—R.

[4] If you get him to admit that *this* is at the bottom of everything, is it therefore at the bottom of everything? All you can say is that you can bring certain people to think that it is.—T.

[5] What does their saying this mean?—T. We could say the same thing against both of them.—R.

[6] But people were immensely attracted by the unity of the theory, by the single principle—which was taken to be the obvious solution. The certainty ('of course') was created by the enormous charm of this unity. People could have said: '. . . Perhaps sometime we shall find grounds.' But hardly anyone said this; they were either sure that it was so, or sure that it was not so.—R.

forget entirely every question of verification, you are just sure it must have been like that.

33. If you are led by psycho-analysis to say that really you thought so and so or that really your motive was so and so, this is not a matter of discovery, but of persuasion.[1] In a different way you could have been persuaded of something different. Of course, if psycho-analysis cures your stammer, it cures it, and that is an achievement. One thinks of certain results of psycho-analysis as a discovery Freud made, as apart from something persuaded to you by a psycho-analyst, and I wish to say this is not the case.

34. Those sentences have the form of persuasion in particular which say 'This is *really* this'. [This means—R] there are certain differences which you have been persuaded to neglect.[2] It reminds me of that marvellous motto: 'Everything is what it is and not another thing.' The dream is not bawdy, it is something else.

35. I very often draw your attention to certain differences, e.g. in these classes I tried to show you that Infinity is not so mysterious as it looks. What I'm doing is also persuasion. If someone says: "There is not a difference", and I say: "There is a difference" I am persuading, I am saying "I don't want you to look at it like that."[3] Suppose I wished to show how very misleading the expressions of Cantor are. You ask: "What do you mean, it is misleading? Where does it lead you to?"

36. Jeans has written a book called *The Mysterious Universe* and I loathe it and call it misleading. Take the title. This alone I would call misleading.[4] Cf. Is the thumb-catcher deluded or not?[5] Was Jeans deluded when he said it was mysterious? I might say the title *The Myterious Universe* includes a kind of idol worship, the idol being Science and the Scientist.

[1] We are likely to think of a person's admitting in analysis that he thought so and so as a kind of discovery which is independent of having been persuaded by a psychoanalyst.—R.

[2] This means you are neglecting certain things and have been persuaded to neglect them.—R.

[3] I am saying I want you to look at the thing in a different way.—T.

[4] But in what way is it misleading? Isn't it mysterious, or is it?—R.

[5] I have been talking about the game of 'thumb catching'. What's wrong with that?—R 'Thumb-catching': holding the right thumb, say, in the left hand, then trying to grasp it with right hand. The thumb 'mysteriously' disappears before it can be grasped.—Ed.

37. I am in a sense making propaganda for one style of thinking as opposed to another. I am honestly disgusted with the other. Also I'm trying to state what I think. Nevertheless I'm saying: "For God's sake don't do this."[1] E.g. I pulled Ursell's proof to bits. But after I had done, he said that the proof had a charm for him. Here I could only say: "It has no charm for me. I loathe it."[2] Cf. the expression 'The Cardinal number of all Cardinal numbers'.

38. Cf. Cantor wrote how marvellous it was that the mathematician could in his imagination [mind—T] transend all limits.

39. I would do my utmost to show it is this charm that makes one do it.[3] Being Mathematics or Physics it looks incontrovertible and this gives it a still greater charm. If we explain the surroundings of the expression we see that the thing could have been expressed in an entirely different way. I can put it in a way in which it will lose its charm for a great number of people and certainly will lose its charm for me.[4]

40. How much we are doing is changing the style of thinking and how much I'm doing is changing the style of thinking and how much I'm doing is persuading people to change their style of thinking.

41. (Much of what we are doing is a question of changing the style of thinking.)

IV

(From Rhees's Notes)

1. Aesthetic puzzles—puzzles about the effects the arts have on us.[5]

Paradigm of the sciences is mechanics. If people imagine a

[1] I stop being puzzled and I persuade you to do something different.—T.

[2] Regarding Cantor's proofs—I would try to show that it is this charm which makes the proof attractive. (After I had discussed these proofs with Ursell, and he had agreed with me, he said: 'And still. . .)—R.

[3] I would do my utmost to show the effects of the charm, and of the associations of 'Mathematics'.—T.

[4] If I describe the surroundings of the proof, then you may see that the thing could have been expressed in an entirely different way; and then you see that the similarity of $\aleph_0$ and a cardinal number is very small. The matter can be put in a way which loses the charm it has for many people.—R.

[5] The puzzles which arise in aesthetics, which are puzzles arising from the effects the arts have, are not puzzles about how these things are caused.—S.

psychology, their ideal is a mechanics of the soul.[1] If we look at what actually corresponds to that, we find there are physical experiments and there are psychological experiments. There are laws of physics and there are laws—if you wish to be polite—of psychology. But in physics there are almost too many laws; in psychology there are hardly any. So, to talk about a mechanics of the soul is slightly funny.

2. But we can dream of predicting the reactions of human beings, say to works of art. If we imagine the dream realized, we'd not thereby have solved what we feel to be aesthetic puzzlements, although we may be able to predict that a certain line of poetry will, on a certain person, act in such and such a way. What we really want, to solve aesthetic puzzlements, is certain comparisons—grouping together of certain cases.[2]

There is a tendency to talk about the 'effect of a work of art'—feelings, images, etc.[3] Then it is natural to ask: "Why do you hear this minuet?", and there is a tendency to answer: "To get this and that effect." And doesn't the minuet itself matter?—hearing *this*: would another have done as well?

You could play a minuet once and get a lot out of it, and play the same minuet another time and get nothing out of it. But it doesn't follow that what you get out of it is then independent of the minuet. Cf. the mistake of thinking that the meaning or thought is just an accompaniment of the word, and the word doesn't matter. 'The sense of a proposition' is very similar to the business of 'an appreciation of art'. The idea that a sentence has a relation to an object, such that, whatever has this effect is the *sense* of the sentence. "What about a French sentence?—There is the same accompaniment, namely the *thought*."

A man may sing a song with expression and without expression. Then why not leave out the song—could you have the expression then?

[1] I suppose the paradigm of all science is mechanics, e.g. Newtonian mechanics. Psychology: Three laws for the soul.—S.

[2] A picture, 'Creation of Adam' by Michelangelo, comes to mind. I have a queer idea which could be expressed by: 'There is a tremendous *philosophy* behind this picture.'—S.

[3] Does that mean that if you gave a person the effects and removed the picture it would be all right? Surely (the) first thing is, you see the picture or say the words of a poem. Would a syringe which produces these effects on you do just as well as the picture?—S.

If a Frenchman says: "It is raining" in French and an Englishman also says it in English, it is not that something happens in both minds which is the real sense of 'It is raining'. We imagine something like *imagery*, which is the international language. Whereas in fact:

(1) Thinking (or imagery) is not an accompaniment of the words as they are spoken or heard;

(2) The sense—the thought 'It's raining'—is not even the words *with* the accompaniment of some sort of imagery.

It *is* the thought 'It's raining' only within the English language.[1]

3. If you ask: "What is the peculiar effect of these words?", in a sense you make a mistake. What if they had no effect at all? Aren't they peculiar words?

"Then why do we admire this and not that?" "I don't know."

Suppose I give you a pill

(1) which makes you draw a picture—perhaps 'The Creation of Adam';

(2) which gives you feelings in the stomach.

Which would you call the more *peculiar* effect? Certainly—that you draw just this picture. The feelings are pretty simple.

"Look at a face—what is important is its expression—not its colour, size, etc."

"Well give us the expression without the face."

The expression is not an *effect* of the face—on me or anyone. You could not say that if anything else had this effect, it would have the expression on this face.[2]

I want to make you sad. I show you a picture, and you are sad. This is the effect of this face.

4. The importance of our memory for the expression of a face. You may show me sticks at different times—one is shorter than the other. I may not remember that the other time it was longer. But I compare them, and this shows me they are not the same.

[1] (You could call the music the scraping of the fiddles, etc., and the effect the noises we hear, but aren't the auditory impressions as important as the visual one?)

Thinking is not even speaking with accompaniment, noises accompanied with whatever may be, is not the sort 'It rains' at all, but is within English language. A Chinaman who makes noise 'It rains' with same accompaniments—Does he think 'It rains'?—S.

[2] Face is not a means to produce the expression.—S.

I may draw you a face. Then at another time I draw another face. You say: "That's not the same face."—but you can't say whether the eyes are closer together, or mouth longer [eyes bigger or nose longer—S], or anything of this sort. "It looks different, somehow."[1]

This is enormously important for all philosophy.

5. If I draw a meaningless curve [squiggle—S]

and then draw another later, pretty much like it, you would not know the difference. But if I draw this peculiar thing which I call a face, and then draw one slightly different, you will know at once there is a difference.

Recognising an expression. Architecture:—draw a door —"Slightly too large." You might say: "He has an excellent eye for measurement." No—he sees it hasn't the right expression—it doesn't make the right gesture.[2]

If you showed me a stick of different length, I'd not have known. Also, in this case I don't make queer gestures and noise; but I do when I see a door or a face.

I say, e.g. of a smile: "It wasn't quite genuine."

"Oh bosh, the lips were parted only 1/1000th of an inch too much. Does it matter?"

"Yes."

"Then it is because of certain consequences."

But not only that: the reaction is different.

We can give the history of the matter—we react so because it is a *human* face. But apart from history—our reaction to these lines is entirely different from our reaction to any other lines. Two faces might have the same expression. Say they are both sad. But if I say: "It has exactly *this* expression. . ." . . ..[3]

[1] It is (the) fact of remembering a facial expression.—S.

[2] Not a matter of measurement.—S.

[3] Can squiggle have same effect as picture of a face? (1) Brothers had same sad expression. (2) It had this expression, photograph and gesture.—S.

6. I draw a few dashes with a pencil and paper, and then ask: "Who is this?" and get the answer: "It is Napoleon". We have never been taught to call these marks, 'Napoleon'.

The phenomenon is similar to that of weighing in a balance.

I can easily distinguish between a few scratches, on the one hand, and a picture of a man properly drawn, on the other. No one would say: "This is the same as that" in one sense. But, on the other hand, we say: "That's Napoleon". On one peculiar [particular?] balance we say: "This is the same as that". On one balance the audience easily distinguishes between the face of the actor and the face of Lloyd George.

All have learnt the use of '='. And suddenly they use it in a peculiar way. They say: "This is Lloyd George," although in another sense there is no similarity. An equality which we could call the 'equality of expression'. We have learnt the use of 'the same'. Suddenly we automatically use 'the same' when there is not similarity of length, weight or anything of the sort.[1]

In a lecture on description Wittgenstein raised another point about similarity which deserves to be quoted and might be included here—Ed. 'Take a case where you notice a peculiarity in poems of one poet. You can sometimes find the similarity between the style of a musician and the style of a poet who lived at the same time, or a painter. Take Brahms and Keller. I often found that certain themes of Brahms were extremely Kellerian. This was extraordinarily striking. First I said this to people. You might say: "What would be the interest of such an utterance?" The interest partly lay in that they lived at the same time.

If I had said he was Shakespearean or Miltonian, this might have had no interest or an entirely different one. If I had constantly wanted to say: "This is Shakespearean" of a certain theme, this would have had little or no interest. It wouldn't connext up with anything. 'This word ('Shakespearean') forces itself on me.' Did I have a certain scene in mind? If I say this theme of Brahms is extremely Kellerian, the interest this has is first that these two lived at the same time. Also that you can say the same sort of things of both of them—the culture of the time in which they lived. If I say this, this comes to an objective interest. The interest might be that my words suggest a hidden connection.

E.g. Here you actually have a case different from that of faces. With faces you can generally soon find something which makes you say: "Yes that's what made them so similar." Whereas I couldn't say now what it is that made Brahms similar to Keller. Nevertheless, I find that utterance of mine interesting. It derives its main interest from the fact that these two lived [at the same time]. "That was [wasn't] written before Wagner." The interest of this statement would lie in the fact that on the whole such statements are true when I make them. One can actually judge when a piece of poetry was written by hearing it, by the style. You could imagine this was impossible, if people in 1850 wrote the same way as in 1750, but you could still imagine people saying: "I am sure that was written in 1850." Cf. [A man on a railway journey to Liverpool saying.] "I am sure Exeter is in that direction." '—S.

[1] We use 'agreed' in another way. This is equality and is equality of expression. We suddenly, automatically, use 'the same' when it's not length, or breadth, etc., although we've learnt it in connection with these.—S.

The most exact description of my feelings here would be that I say: "Oh, that's Lloyd George!"[1]

Suppose the most exact description of a feeling is "stomach-ache". But why isn't the most important description of feeling that you say: "Oh, this is the same as that!"?

7. Here is the point of Behaviorism. It isn't that they deny there are feelings. But they say our description of behaviour *is* our description of feelings.

"What did he feel when he said: 'Duncan is in his grave'?" Can I describe his feelings better than by describing how he said it?[2] All other descriptions are crude compared with a description of the gesture he made, the tone of voice with which he made it.

What is a description of feeling at all? What is a description of pain?[3]

Discussion of a comedian doing imitations, sketches. Suppose you want to describe the experience of the audience—why not describe first of all what they saw? Then perhaps that they shook with laughter, then what they said.[4]

"This can't be a description of their feelings." One says this because one is thinking of their organic feelings—tension of the muscles in their chest, etc. This would obviously be an experience. But it doesn't seem half as important as the fact that they said so and so. One thinks of a description of experience not as a description of action, but as of a description of pain or organic feelings.

Cf. what we said about the way in which fashions arise: whether he feels so and so when he cuts lapel of coat bigger. But that he *cuts* it in this way, etc.[5]—this is the most important part of the experience.

[1] Important thing is I say: 'Yes, this is Drury.' If you wish to describe feelings, the best way is to describe reactions. Saying 'This is Drury' is the most exact description of feelings I can give at all. Idea that most exact way of describing is by feelings in the stomach.—S.

[2] Can I describe his feelings better than (by) imitating the way he said it? Isn't this most impressive?—S.

[3] 'He felt this' (touching head).—S.

[4] Suppose I said: 'The crowd roared with laughter,' without describing what they were laughing at; describing what they were laughing at but not them laughing. Why not first describe what they saw, then what they did or said, then feelings?—S.

[5] . . . his making it bigger or saying: 'No, no, no?'—S.

8. "Is the most important impression which a picture produces a visual impression or not?"

[(1)] "No. Because you can do things which visually change the picture and yet not change the impression." This sounds as though one wished to say it wasn't an impression of the eyes: an effect, but not a purely visual effect.

[(2)] "But it *is* a visual impression". Only these are the features of the visual impression which matter, and not the others.

Suppose [someone says]: "Associations are what matter —change it slightly and it no longer has the same associations."

But can you separate the associations from the picture, and have the same thing? You can't say: "That's just as good as the other: it gives me the same associations."

9. You *could* select either of two poems to remind you of death, say. But supposing you had read a poem and admired it, could you say: "Oh, read the other it will do the same"?

How do we use poetry? Does it play this role—that we say such a thing as: "Here is something just as good. . . ."?

Imagine an entirely different civilization.[1] Here there is something you might call music, since it has notes. They treat music like this: certain music makes them walk like this. They play a record to do this. One says: "I need this record now. Oh no, take the other, it is just as good."

If I admire a minuet I can't say: "Take another. It does the same thing." What do you mean? It *is* not the same.[2]

If someone talks bosh, imagine a case in which it is not bosh. The moment you imagine it, you see at once it is not like that in our case. We *don't* read poetry to get associations. We don't happen to, but we might.

10. Two schools:

(1) "What matters is the patches of colour [and lines—S]."

(2) "What matters is the expression on these faces."

In a sense, these two don't contradict one another. Only (1) doesn't make clear that the different patches have different

[1]Another culture where music makes them do different things. Cf. (the) rôle music plays with us with the rôle music plays with others. One can't say now: 'Play Mozart it does just as well.'—S.

[2] Cf. language where producing pictures by words is important thing. You can see how our language is not like that.

Poems, sea, sea-picture. Ask him. Show him the difference, etc.—S.

importance, and that different *alterations* have totally different effects: some make all the difference in the world.

"A picture must be good even if you look at it upside down." Then, the smile may not be noticeable.

[Suppose you said:] "That tiny smile by which you change the kindly smile into an ironic one, is not a purely visual difference," (Cf. a picture of a monk looking at a vision of the Virgin Mary.) [Suppose you said:] "It changes your whole attitude towards the picture." This may be entirely true. How would this be expressed? Perhaps by the smile you make. The one picture might be blasphemous; with the other you are as you might be in a church. Your attitude might be in the one case that you stand before it almost in prayer, in the other case almost leering. This is a difference of attitude.

"Well, there you are. It is all the attitude." But you could have these attitudes without a picture. They are important—certainly.

11. "You have given a rough description of the attitude. What you have to describe is something more subtle." But if we describe the attitude more exactly, how do you know that this is the essential thing for *this* picture—that all this must always be present?

Don't imagine a description which you have never heard, which describes an attitude in unheard of detail. For you know nothing about such an attitude. We have no idea of such an attitude.

An attitude is pretty well described by the position of the body. This is a good description. But accurate? In a way it is inaccurate. "But if you knew all the muscular sensations, you would point to just those which matter."[1] I don't know them and I don't know what such a description would be like.[2] This is not what we mean by description. Don't imagine an imaginary kind of description of which you really have no idea.

If you say 'description of attitude', tell us what you call a description of attitude, then you will see the attitude matters. Some changes change the attitude—We say: "the whole thing is changed."

[1]Who says he always must have this feeling in this muscle? He distinguishes between looking at the picture and looking at this, but he does not distinguish between his muscular feelings.—S.

[2] I can describe how a man stands and then I can describe the picture. Man who makes twelve changes in Michaelangelo.—S.

12. Associations also [enormously] matter. These are shown chiefly by the things we say. We call this 'God the Father', the other 'Adam'; we could go on: "That comes in the Bible, etc." Is this all that matters? We could have all these associations with a different picture, and would still want to see *this* picture.

"That means the chief impression is the visual impression." Yes, it's the picture which seems to matter most. Associations may vary, attitudes may vary, but change the picture ever so slightly, and you won't want to look at it any more.

The craving for simplicity. [People would like to say:] "What really matters is only the colours." You say this mostly because you wish it to be the case. If your explanation is complicated, it is disagreeable, especially if you don't have strong feelings about the thing itself.

FROM A LECTURE BELONGING TO A COURSE OF LECTURES ON DESCRIPTION

One of the most interesting points which the question of not being able to describe is connected with, [is that] the impression which a certain verse or bar in music gives you is indescribable. "I don't know what it is. . . Look at this transition. . . . What is it? . . ." I think you would say it gives you experiences which can't be described. First of all it is, of course, not true that whenever we hear a piece of music or a line of poetry which impresses us greatly, we say: "This is indescribable". But it is true that again and again we do feel inclined to say: "I can't describe my experience". I have in mind a case that saying one is incapable of describing comes from being intrigued and *wanting* to describe, asking oneself: "What is this? What's he doing, wanting to do here?—Gosh, if I could only say what he's doing here."

Very many people have the feeling: "I can make a gesture but that's all". One example is that you say of a certain phrase of music that it draws a conclusion, "Though I couldn't say for my life why it is a 'therefore'!" You say in this case that it is indescribable. But this does not mean that you may not one day say that something is a *description*. You may one day find the *word* or you find a verse that fits it. "It is as though he said: ' . . .'," and you have a verse. And now perhaps you say: "And now I understand it."

If you say: "We haven't got the technique" (I. A. Richards), what in such a case are we entitled to call such a description? You might say some such thing as: "Well, now, if you hear this piece of music, you get certain sense impressions. Certain images, certain organic feelings, emotions, etc.", meanings, "we still don't know how to analyse this impression."

The mistake seems to me in the idea of description. I said before, with some people, me especially, the expression of an emotion in music, say, is a certain gesture. If I make a certain gesture. . . . "It is quite obvious that you have certain kinesthetic feelings. It means to you certain kinesthetic feelings." Which ones? How can you describe them? Except, perhaps, just by the gesture?

Suppose you said: "This phrase in music always makes me make one peculiar gesture." A painter might draw this gesture. A man, instead of making a gesture, would draw a gesture. For him it would be an expression to draw this gesture, or a face going with it, as for me it is to make a gesture. "Wittgenstein, you talk as if this phrase gave you sensations you couldn't describe. All you get is sensations in your muscles." This is utterly misleading. We look up muscles in a book on anatomy, we press certain parts and give these sensations names, 'A', 'B', 'C', etc. All that would be needed for a piece of music would be the description 'A', etc., giving the sensations in each muscle. It now seems as though you could do something like this. What a man sees can generally be described. Names of colours etc. One assumes at least a picture can be described. One goes on and says not only a visual picture but picture of Kinesthetic Sensations.

By the way, in what way is it wrong for a picture? Suppose we said, that we cannot describe in words the expression of God in Michelangelo's 'Adam'. "But this is only a matter of technique, because if we drew a lattice-work over his face, numbered,

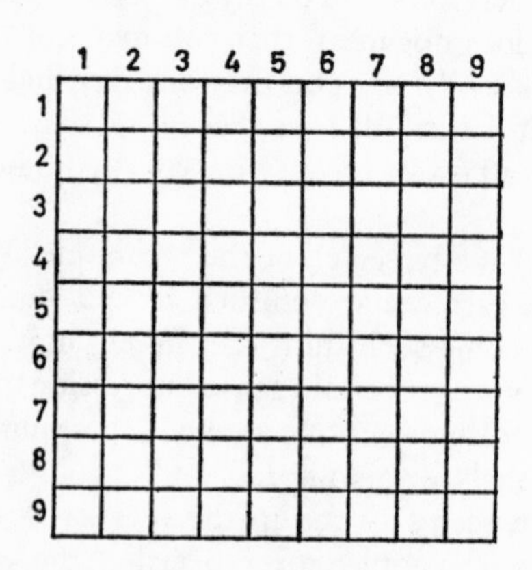

I would just write down numbers and you might say: "My God! It's grand." It wouldn't be any description. You wouldn't say

such a thing at all. It would only be a description if you could paint (act?) according to this picture, which, of course, is conceivable. But this would show that you can't at all transmit the impression by words, but you'd have again to paint.

Could you imagine: it is an odd fact that we sometimes imitate someone else? I remember walking in the street and saying: "I am now walking exactly like Russell." You might say it was a kinesthetic sensation. Very queer.

A person who imitates another's face doesn't do it before a mirror but it is a fact that there is such a thing as saying: "The face is so and so."

Suppose I make a gesture and I think the gesture characteristic for the impression I get. Suppose I gave the gesture by co-ordinates and I wish to make it clear to Mr. Lewy. He might have to make an analogous gesture. His muscles, hands, etc., are differently shaped. So in one sense, he can't copy and in another sense he can. What are we to regard as the copy? "It will depend on how such muscles contract." But how on earth are you to know? If I make a gesture, and you are good imitators, these gestures will have to be similar, but different; the shape of the fingers, etc., is different. The criterion for its being this gesture will be the clicking of it in you. You say: "Now this." To say what's similar is impossible (to say). Each one makes a gesture immediately and says: "That's the one."

If I wish to convey an impression to Mr. Lewy, it might only be made in this way, that he copies my gesture. Then what about this technique of describing kinesthetic sensations? This isn't coordinates; it is something else: imitating the person. "Wittgenstein, if you make a gesture, all you get are certain kinesthetic sensations." It is not at all clear in what case we do say we have conveyed them. But it may, e.g., be by what we call 'imitating'.

Whether it is this will depend on. . . .

"There is a phenomenon, the following: if you give me a piece of music and ask me in what tempo it ought to be played, I may or may not be absolutely certain. "Perhaps, like this . . . I don't know." Or "Like this", telling you exactly what tempo it is to be. I always insist on one tempo, not necessarily the same. In the other case I am uncertain. Suppose the question were to transmit to you a certain impression I get of a piece of music. That might depend on the fact that a certain number of you, on my playing it to you, (that you) "get it", 'get hold of it'. What does it consist in to get hold of a tune or a piece of poetry?

You may read a stanza. I let you all read it. Everyone reads it slightly differently. I get the definite impression that "None of them has got hold of it." Suppose then I read it out to you and say: "Look, this is how it ought to be". Then four of you read this stanza, no one exactly like the other, but in such a way that I say: "Each one is exactly certain of himself." This is a phenomenon, being certain of yourself, reading it in *one way only*. He is absolutely exact as to what pause to make. I might say in this case that you four have got hold of it. I would have conveyed something to you. I would perfectly correctly say, that I have exactly conveyed to you the exact experience I had.

But what about the technique of imagery, etc.? This (convention/communication/description) is not based on copying me exactly. If I had a chronometer by which I can measure exactly the interval between the vowels, they may not be the same but entirely different.

If someone says: "We lack this technique", he presupposes that, if we had it, we would have a new expression, a new way of transmitting, not the old one. But how does he know that if we describe in the new way—suppose I had a way of describing kinesthetic sensations or way of describing gestures—I get the same as I got if I transmit gesture. Suppose I said: "I get a little tickling there" [running finger down hand]. Suppose I had six ticklings and I had a method of producing each one. Suppose I had instruments attached to my nerves in such a way that an electric current going through the nerves was measured by the instrument. You get an instrument reading. "Now I'll represent this in Mr. Lewy." But would this be the representation we want? I might read a stanza and you might say: "Wittgenstein obviously has got hold of it. He had got my interpretation." Mr. Lewy reads it and you say the same. But voice, strength, etc., are different. "My interpretation is that which produces the same kinesthetic impressions." But how do you know? This simply isn't an analysis at all. We have one way of comparing and if you say: "And also we could get a scientific one," I'd ask: "Yes, but what makes you think that these will go parallel at all?"

CONVERSATIONS ON FREUD

In these discussions Wittgenstein was critical of Freud. But he was also bringing out how much there is in what Freud says about the notion of "dream symbolism", for instance, or the suggestion that in dreaming I am—in some sense—'saying something'. He was trying to separate what is valuable in Freud from that 'way of thinking' which he wanted to combat.

He told me that when he was in Cambridge before 1914 he had thought psychology a waste of time. (Although he had not ignored it. I heard him explain the Weber-Fechner law to a student in a way that cannot have come simply from reading Meinong's article or from discussions with Russell.) "Then some years later I happened to read something by Freud, and I sat up in surprise. Here was someone who had something to say." I think this was soon after 1919. And for the rest of his life Freud was one of the few authors he thought worth reading. He would speak of himself—at the period of these discussions—as "a disciple of Freud" and "a follower of Freud".

He admired Freud for the observations and suggestions in his writings; for "having something to say" even where, in Wittgenstein's view, he was wrong. On the other hand, he thought the enormous influence of psychoanalysis in Europe and America was harmful—"although it will take a long time before we lose our subservience to it". To learn from Freud you have to be critical; and psychoanalysis generally prevents this.

I spoke of the harm it does to writing when an author tries to bring psychoanalysis into the story. "Of course," he said, "There's nothing worse." He was ready to illustrate what Freud meant by referring to a story; but then the story had been written independently. Once when Wittgenstein was recounting something Freud had said and the advice he had given someone, one of us said that this advice did not seem very wise. "Oh certainly not," said Wittgenstein. "But wisdom is something I never would expect from Freud. Cleverness, certainly; but not wisdom." Wisdom was something he did admire in his favourite story writers—in Gottfried Keller, for instance. The kind of criticism which would help in studying Freud, would have to go deep; and it is not common.

RUSH RHEES.

WITTGENSTEIN (notes by R. R. after a conversation, Summer 1942).

When we are studying psychology we may feel there is something unsatisfactory, some difficulty about the whole subject or study—because we are taking physics as our ideal science. We think of formulating laws as in physics. And then we find we cannot use the same sort of 'metric', the same ideas of measurement as in physics. This is especially clear when we try to describe appearances: the least noticeable differences of colours; the least noticeable differences of length, and so on. Here it seems that we cannot say: "If A=B, and B=C, then A=C," for instance. And this sort of trouble goes all through the subject.

Or suppose you want to speak of causality in the operation of feelings. "Determinism applies to the mind as truly as to physical things." This is obscure because when we think of causal laws in physical things we think of *experiments*. We have nothing like this in connexion with feelings and motivation. And yet psychologists wants to say: "There *must* be some law"—although no law has been found. (Freud: "Do you want to say, gentlemen, that changes in mental phenomena are guided by *chance*?") Whereas to me the fact that there *aren't* actually any such laws seems important.

Freud's theory of dreams. He wants to say that whatever happens in a dream will be found to be connected with some wish which analysis can bring to light. But this procedure of free association and so on is queer, because Freud never shows how we know where to stop—where is the right solution. Sometimes he says that the right solution, or the right analysis, is the one which satisfies the patient. Sometimes he says that the doctor knows what the right solution or analysis of the dream is whereas the patient doesn't: the doctor can say that the patient is wrong.

The reason why he calls one sort of analysis the right one, does not seem to be a matter of evidence. Neither is the proposition that hallucinations, and so dreams, are wish fulfilments.

Suppose a starving man has an hallucination of food. Freud wants to say the hallucination of anything requires tremendous energy: it is not something that could normally happen, but the energy is provided in the exceptional circumstances where a man's wish for food is overpowering. This is a *speculation*. It is the sort of explanation we are inclined to accept. It is not put forward as a result of detailed examination of varieties of hallucinations.

Freud in his analysis provides explanations which many people are inclined to accept. He emphasizes that people are *dis*-inclined to accept them. But if the explanation is one which people are disinclined to accept, it is highly probable that it is also one which they are *inclined* to accept. And this is what Freud had actually brought out. Take Freud's view that anxiety is always a repetition in some way of the anxiety we felt at birth. He does not establish this by reference to evidence—for he could not do so. But it is an idea which has a marked attraction. It has the attraction which mythological explanations have, explanations which say that this is all a repetition of something that has happened before. And when people do accept or adopt this, then certain things seem much clearer and easier for them. So it is with the notion of the unconscious also. Freud does claim to find evidence in memories brought to light in analysis. But at a certain stage it is not clear how far such memories are due to the analyst. In any case, do they show that the anxiety was necessarily a repetition of the original anxiety?

Symbolizing in dreams. The idea of a dream language. Think of recognizing a painting as a dream. I (L.W.) was once looking at an exhibition of paintings by a young woman artist in Vienna. There was one painting of a bare room, like a cellar. Two men in top hats were sitting on chairs. Nothing else. And the title: "Besuch" ("Visit"). When I saw this I said at once "This is a dream", (My sister described the picture to Freud, and he said 'Oh yes, that is quite a common dream'—connected with virginity.) Note that the the title is what clinches it as a dream—by which I do not mean that anything like this was dreamt by the painter while asleep. You would not say of *every* painting 'This is a dream'. And this does show that there is something like a dream language.

Freud mentions various symbols: top hats are regularly phallic symbols, wooden things like tables are women, etc. His historical explanation of these symbols is absurd. We might say it is not needed anyway: it is the most natural thing in the world that a table should be that sort of symbol.

But dreaming—using this sort of language—although it *may* be used to refer to a woman or to a phallus, may *also* be used not to refer to that at all. If some activity is shown to be carried out often for a certain purpose—striking someone to inflict pain—then a hundred to one it is also carried out under other circumstances *not* for that purpose. He may just want to strike him without thinking of inflicting pain at all. The fact that we are inclined to recognize the hat as a phallic symbol does not mean that the artist was necessarily referring to a phallus in any way when she painted it.

Consider the difficulty that if a symbol in a dream is not understood, it does not seem to be a symbol at all. So why call it one? But suppose I have a dream and accept a certain interpretation of it. *Then*—when I superimpose the interpretation on the dream—I can say "Oh yes, the table obviously corresponds to the woman, this to that etc."

I might be making scratches on the wall. It seems in a way like writing, but it is not a writing which either I or anyone else would recognize or understand. So we say I'm doodling. Then an analyst begins to ask me questions, trace associations and so on; and we come to an explanation of why I'm doing this. We may then correlate various scratches which I make with various elements in the interpretation. And we may then refer to the doodling as a kind of writing, as using a kind of language, although it was not understood by anyone.

Freud is constantly claiming to be scientific. But what he gives is *speculation*—something prior even to the formation of an hypothesis.

He speaks of overcoming resistance. One "instance" is deluded by another "instance". (In the sense in which we speak of "a court of higher instance" with authority to overrule the judgment of the lower court. RR.) The analyst is supposed to be stronger, able to combat and overcome the delusion of the instance. But there is no way of showing that the whole result of analysis may not be "delusion". It is something which people are inclined to accept and which makes it easier for them to go certain ways:

it makes certain ways of behaving and thinking natural for them. They have given up one way of thinking and adopted another.

Can we say we have laid bare the essential nature of mind? "Concept formation". Couldn't the whole thing have been differently treated?

WITTGENSTEIN (notes following conversations in 1943; Rush Rhees).

DREAMS. The interpretation of dreams. Symbolism.

When Freud speaks of certain images—say the image of a hat—as symbols, or when he says the image "means" so and so, he is speaking of interpretation; and of what the dreamer can be brought to accept as an interpretation.

It is characteristic of dreams that often they seem to the dreamer to call for an interpretation. One is hardly ever inclined to write down a day dream, or recount it to someone else, or to ask "What does it mean?" But dreams do seem to have something puzzling and in a special way interesting about them—so that we want an interpretation of them. (They were often regarded as messages.)

There seems to be something in dream images that has a certain resemblance to the signs of a language. As a series of marks on paper or on sand might have. There might be no mark which we recognized as a conventional sign in any alphabet we knew, and yet we might have a strong feeling that they must be a language of some sort: that they mean something. There is a cathedral in Moscow with five spires. On each of these there is a different sort of curving configuration. One gets the strong impression that these different shapes and arrangements must mean something.

When a dream is interpreted we might say that it is fitted into a context in which it ceases to be puzzling. In a sense the dreamer re-dreams his dream in surroundings such that its aspect changes. It is as though we were presented with a bit of canvas on which were painted a hand and a part of a face and certain other shapes, arranged in a puzzling and incongruous manner. Suppose this bit is surrounded by considerable stretches of blank canvas, and that we now paint in forms—say an arm, a trunk, etc.—leading up to and fitting on to the shapes on the original bit; and that the result is that we say: "Ah, now I see why it is like that, how it all comes to be arranged in that way, and what these various bits are . . ." and so on.

Mixed up with the shapes on the original bit of canvas there might be certain forms of which we should say that they do not join on to further figures in the wider canvas; they are not parts of bodies or trees, etc., but bits of writing. We might say this of a snake, perhaps, or a hat or some such. (These would be like the configurations of the Moscow cathedral.)

What is done in interpreting dreams is not all of one sort. There is a work of interpretation which, so to speak, still belongs to the dream itself. In considering what a dream is, it is important to consider what happens to it, the way its aspect changes when it is brought into relation with other things remembered, for instance. On first awaking a dream may impress one in various ways. One may be terrified and anxious; or when one has written the dream down one may have a certain sort of thrill, feel a very lively interest in it, feel intrigued by it. If one now remembers certain events in the previous day and connects what was dreamed with these, this already makes a difference, changes the aspect of the dream. If reflecting on the dream then leads one to remember certain things in early childhood, this will give it a different aspect still. And so on. (All this is connected with what was said about dreaming the dream over again. It still belongs to the dream, in a way.)

On the other hand, one might form an hypothesis. On reading the report of the dream, one might predict that the dreamer can be brought to recall such and such memories. And this hypothesis might or might not be verified. This might be called a scientific treatment of the dream.

Freier Einfall and wish fulfilments. There are various criteria for the right interpretation: e.g., (1) what the analyst says or predicts, on the basis of his previous experience; (2) what the dreamer is led to by *freier Einfall*. It would be interesting and important if these two generally coincided. But it would be queer to claim (as Freud seems to) that they *must always* coincide.

What goes on in *freier Einfall* is probably conditioned by a whole host of circumstances. There seems to be no reason for saying that it must be conditioned only by the sort of wish in which the analyst is interested and of which he has reason to say that it must have been playing a part. If you want to complete what seems to be a fragment of a picture, you might be advised to give up trying to think hard about what is the most likely way the picture went, and instead simply to stare at the picture and make whatever dash first comes into your mind, without thinking. This might in many cases be very fruitful advice to give. But it would be astonishing if it *always* produced the best results. What dashes you make, is likely to be conditioned by everything that is going on about you and within you. And if I knew one of the factors present, this could not tell me with certainty what dash you were going to make.

To say that dreams are wish fulfilments is very important chiefly because it points to the sort of interpretation that is wanted —the sort of thing that would be an interpretation of a dream. As contrasted with an interpretation which said that dreams were simply memories of what had happened, for instance. (We don't feel that memories call for an interpretation in the same way as we feel this about dreams.) And some dreams obviously are wish fulfilments; such as the sexual dreams of adults, for instance. But it seems muddled to say that *all* dreams are hallucinated wish fulfilments. (Freud very commonly gives what we might call a sexual interpretation. But it is interesting that among all the reports of dreams which he gives, there is not a single example of a straightforward sexual dream. Yet these are common as rain.) Partly because this doesn't seem to fit with dreams that spring from fear rather than from longing. Partly because the majority of dreams Freud considers have to be regarded as *camouflaged* wish fulfilments; and in this case they simply don't fulfil the wish. Ex hypothesi the wish is not allowed to be fulfilled, and something else is hallucinated instead. If the wish is cheated in this way, then the dream can hardly be called a fulfilment of it. Also it becomes impossible to say whether it is the wish or the censor that is cheated. Apparently both are, and the result is that neither is satisfied. So that, the dream is not an hallucinated satisfaction of anything.

It is probable that there are many different sorts of dreams, and that there is no single line of explanation for all of them. Just as there are many different sorts of jokes. Or just as there are many different sorts of language.

Freud was influenced by the 19th century idea of dynamics—an idea which has influenced the whole treatment of psychology. He wanted to find some one explanation which would show what dreaming is. He wanted to find the *essence* of dreaming. And he would have rejected any suggestion that he might be partly right but not altogether so. If he was partly wrong, that would have meant for him that he was wrong altogether—that he had not really found the essence of dreaming.

WITTGENSTEIN. (Notes following conversations, 1943. R.R.)

Whether a dream is a thought. Whether dreaming is thinking about something.

Suppose you look on a dream as a kind of language. A way of saying something, or a way of symbolizing something. There might be a regular symbolism, not necessarily alphabetical—it might be like Chinese, say. We might then find a way of translating this symbolism into the language of ordinary speech, ordinary thoughts. But then the translation ought to be possible both ways. It ought to be possible by employing the same technique to translate ordinary thoughts into dream language. As Freud recognizes, this never is done and cannot be done. So we might question whether dreaming is a way of thinking something, whether it is a language at all.

Obviously there are certain similarities with language.

Suppose there were a picture in a comic paper, dated shortly after the last war. It might contain one figure of which you would say it was obviously a caricature of Churchill, another figure marked somehow with a hammer and sickle so that you would say it was obviously supposed to be Russia. Suppose the title of the picture was lacking. Still you might be sure that, in view of two figures mentioned, the whole picture was obviously trying to make some point about the political situation at that time.

The question is whether you would always be justified in assuming that there is some one joke or some one point which is *the* point which the cartoon is making. Perhaps even the picture as a whole has no "right interpretation" at all. You might say:

"There are indications—such as the two figures mentioned—which suggest that it has." And I might answer that perhaps these indications are all that there is. Once you have got an interpretation of these two figures, there may be no ground for saying that there *must* be an interpretation of the whole thing or of every detail of it on similar lines.

The situation may be similar in dreams.

Freud would ask: "What made you hallucinate that situation at all?" One might answer that there need not have been anything that *made* me hallucinate it.

Freud seems to have certain prejudices about when an interpretation could be regarded as complete—and so about when it still requires completion, when further interpretation is needed. Suppose someone were ignorant of the tradition among sculptors of making busts. If he then came upon the finished bust of some man, he might say that obviously this is a fragment and that there must have been other parts belonging to it, making it a whole body.

Suppose you recognized certain things in the dream which can be interpreted in the Freudian manner. Is there any ground at all for assuming that there must be an interpretation for everything else in the dream as well? that it makes any sense to ask what is the right interpretation of the other things there?

Freud asks "Are you asking me to believe that there is anything which happens without a cause?" But this means nothing. If under 'cause' you include things like physiological causes, then we know nothing about these, and in any case they are not relevant to the question of interpretation. Certainly you can't argue from Freud's question to the proposition that everything in the dream must have a cause in the sense of some past event with which it is connected by association in that way.

Suppose we were to regard a dream as a kind of game which the dreamer played. (And by the way, there is no one cause or one reason why children always play. This is where theories of play generally go wrong.) There might be a game in which paper figures were put together to form a story, or at any rate were somehow assembled. The materials might be collected and stored in a scrap-book, full of pictures and anecdotes. The child might then take various bits from the scrap-book to put into the construction; and he might take a considerable picture because it had something in it which he wanted and he might just include the rest because it was there.

Compare the question of why we dream and why we write stories. Not everything in the story is allegorical. What would be meant by trying to explain why he has written just that story in just that way?

There is no one reason why people talk. A small child babbles often just for the pleasure of making noises. This is also one reason why adults talk. And there are countless others.

Freud seems constantly to be influenced by the thought that a hallucination is something requiring a tremendous mental force—*seelische Kraft*. 'Ein Traum findet sich niemals mit Halbheiten ab.' And he thinks that the only force strong enough to produce the hallucinations of dreams is to be found in the deep wishes of early childhood. One might question this. Supposing it is true that hallucinations in waking state require an extraordinary mental force—why should not dream hallucinations be the perfectly normal thing in sleep, not requiring any extraordinary force at all?

(Compare the question: "Why do we punish criminals? Is it from a desire for revenge? Is it in order to prevent a repetition of the crime?" And so on. The truth is that there is no one reason. There is the institution of punishing criminals. Different people support this for different reasons, and for different reasons in different cases and at different times. Some people support it out of a desire for revenge, some perhaps out of a desire for justice, some out of a wish to prevent a repetition of the crime, and so on. And so punishments are carried out.)

WITTGENSTEIN (notes following conversation, 1946 R.R.)

I have been going through Freud's "Interpretation of Dreams" with H. And it has made me feel how much this whole way of thinking wants combatting.

If I take any one of the dream reports (reports of his own dreams) which Freud gives, I can by the use of free association arrive at the same results as those he reaches in his analysis—although it was not my dream. And the association will proceed through my own experiences and so on.

The fact is that whenever you are preoccupied with something, with some trouble or with some problem which is a big thing in your life—as sex is, for instance—then no matter what you start from, the association will lead finally and inevitably back to that same theme. Freud remarks on how, after the analysis of it, the dream appears so very logical. And of course it does.

You could start with any of the objects on this table—which certainly are not put there through your dream activity—and you could find that they all could be connected in a pattern like that; and the pattern would be logical in the same way.

One may be able to discover certain things about oneself by this sort of free association, but it does not explain why the dream occurred.

Freud refers to various ancient myths in these connexions, and claims that his researches have now explained how it came about that anybody should think or propound a myth of that sort.

Whereas in fact Freud has done something different. He has not given a scientific explanation of the ancient myth. What he has done is to propound a new myth. The attractiveness of the suggestion, for instance, that all anxiety is a repetition of the anxiety of the birth trauma, is just the attractiveness of a mythology. "It is all the outcome of something that happened long ago." Almost like referring to a totem.

Much the same could be said of the notion of an 'Urszene'. This often has the attractiveness of giving a sort of tragic pattern to one's life. It is all the repetition of the same pattern which was settled long ago. Like a tragic figure carrying out the decrees under which the fates had placed him at birth. Many people have, at some period, serious trouble in their lives—so serious as to lead to thoughts of suicide. This is likely to appear to one as something nasty, as a situation which is too foul to be a subject of a tragedy. And it may then be an immense relief if it can be shown that one's life has the pattern rather of a tragedy—the tragic working out and repetition of a pattern which was determined by the primal scene.

There is of course the difficulty of determining what scene is the primal scene—whether it is the scene which the patient recognizes as such, or whether it is the one whose recollection effects the cure. In practice these criteria are mingled together.

Analysis is likely to do harm. Because although one may

discover in the course of it various things about oneself, one must have a very strong and keen and persistent criticism in order to recognize and see through the mythology that is offered or imposed on one. There is an inducement to say, 'Yes, of course, it must be like that'. A powerful mythology.

LECTURES ON RELIGIOUS BELIEF

I

An Austrian general said to someone: "I shall think of you after my death, if that should be possible." We can imagine one group who would find this ludicrous, another who wouldn't.

(During the war, Wittgenstein saw consecrated bread being carried in chromium steel. This struck him as ludicrous.)

Suppose that someone believed in the Last Judgement, and I don't, does this mean that I believe the opposite to him, just that there won't be such a thing? I would say: "not at all, or not always."

Suppose I say that the body will rot, and another says "No. Particles will rejoin in a thousand years, and there will be a Resurrection of you."

If some said: "Wittgenstein, do you believe in this?" I'd say: "No." "Do you contradict the man?" I'd say: "No."

If you say this, the contradiction already lies in this.

Would you say: "I believe the opposite", or "There is no reason to suppose such a thing"? I'd say neither.

Suppose someone were a believer and said: "I believe in a Last Judgement," and I said: "Well, I'm not so sure. Possibly." You would say that there is an enormous gulf between us. If he said "There is a German aeroplane overhead," and I said "Possibly I'm not so sure," you'd say we were fairly near.

It isn't a question of my being anywhere near him, but on an entirely different plane, which you could express by saying: "You mean something altogether different, Wittgenstein."

The difference might not show up at all in any explanation of the meaning.

Why is it that in this case I seem to be missing the entire point?

Suppose somebody made this guidance for this life: believing in the Last Judgment. Whenever he does anything, this is before his mind. In a way, how are we to know whether to say he believes this will happen or not?

Asking him is not enough. He will probably say he has proof.

But he has what you might call an unshakeable belief. It will show, not by reasoning or by appeal to ordinary grounds for belief, but rather by regulating for in all his life.

This is a very much stronger fact—foregoing pleasures, always appealing to this picture. This is one sense must be called the firmest of all beliefs, because the man risks things on account of it which he would not do on things which are by far better established for him. Although he distinguishes between things well-established and not well-established.

Lewy: Surely, he would say it is extremely well-established.

First, he may use "well-established" or not use it at all. He will treat this belief as extremely well-established, and in another way as not well-established at all.

If we have a belief, in certain cases we appeal again and again to certain grounds, and at the same time we risk pretty little—if it came to risking our lives on the ground of this belief.

There are instances where you have a faith—where you say "I believe"—and on the other hand this belief does not rest on the fact on which our ordinary everyday beliefs normally do rest.

How should we compare beliefs with each other? What would it mean to compare them?

You might say: 'We compare the states of mind."

How do we compare states of mind? This obviously won't do for all occasions. First, what you say won't be taken as the measure for the firmness of a belief? But, for instance, what risks you would take?

The strength of a belief is not comparable with the intensity of a pain.

An entirely different way of comparing beliefs is seeing what sorts of grounds he will give.

A belief isn't like a momentary state of mind. "At 5 o'clock he had very bad toothache."

Suppose you had two people, and one of them, when he had to decide which course to take, thought of retribution, and the other did not. One person might, for instance, be inclined to take everything that happened to him as a reward or punishment, and another person doesn't think of this at all.

If he is ill, he may think: "What have I done to deserve this?" This is one way of thinking of retribution. Another way is, he thinks in a general way whenever he is ashamed of himself: "This will be punished."

Take two people, one of whom talks of his behaviour and of what happens to him in terms of retribution, the other one does not. These people think entirely differently. Yet, so far, you can't say they believe different things.

Suppose someone is ill and he says: "This is a punishment," and I say: "If I'm ill, I don't think of punishment at all." If you say: "Do you believe the opposite?"—you can call it believing the opposite, but it is entirely different from what we would normally call believing the opposite.

I think differently, in a different way. I say different things to myself. I have different pictures.

It is this way: if someone said: "Wittgenstein, you don't take illness as punishment, so what do you believe?"—I'd say: "I don't have any thoughts of punishment."

There are, for instance, these entirely different ways of thinking first of all—which needn't be expressed by one person saying one thing, another person another thing.

What we call believing in a Judgement Day or not believing in a Judgement Day—The expression of belief may play an absolutely minor role.

If you ask me whether or not I believe in a Judgement Day, in the sense in which religious people have belief in it, I wouldn't say: "No. I don't believe there will be such a thing." It would seem to me utterly crazy to say this.

And then I give an explanation: "I don't believe in . . .", but then the religious person never believes what I describe.

I can't say. I can't contradict that person.

In one sense, I understand all he says—the English words "God", "separate", etc. I understand. I could say: "I don't believe in this," and this would be true, meaning I haven't got these thoughts or anything that hangs together with them. But not that I could contradict the thing.

You might say: "Well, if you can't contradict him, that means you don't understand him. If you did understand him, then you might." That again is Greek to me. My normal technique of language leaves me. I don't know whether to say they understand one another or not.

These controversies look quite different from any normal controversies. Reasons look entirely different from normal reasons.

They are, in a way, quite inconclusive.

The point is that if there were evidence, this would in fact destroy the whole business.

Anything that I normally call evidence wouldn't in the slightest influence me.

Suppose, for instance, we knew people who foresaw the future; make forecasts for years and years ahead; and they described some sort of a Judgement Day. Queerly enough, even if there were such a thing, and even if it were more convincing than I have described but, belief in this happening wouldn't be at all a religious belief.

Suppose that I would have to forego all pleasures because of such a forecast. If I do so and so, someone will put me in fires in a thousand years, etc. I wouldn't budge. The best scientific evidence is just nothing.

A religious belief might in fact fly in the face of such a forecast, and say "No. There it will break down."

As it were, the belief as formulated on the evidence can only be the last result—in which a number of ways of thinking and acting crystallize and come together.

A man would fight for his life not to be dragged into the fire. No induction. Terror. That is, as it were, part of the substance of the belief.

That is partly why you don't get in religious controversies, the form of controversy where one person is *sure* of the thing, and the other says: 'Well, possibly.'

You might be surprised that there hasn't been opposed to those who believe in Resurrection those who say "Well, possibly."

Here believing obviously plays much more this role: suppose we said that a certain picture might play the role of constantly admonishing me, or I always think of it. Here, an enormous difference would be between those people for whom the picture is constantly in the foreground, and the others who just didn't use it at all.

Those who said: "Well, possibly it may happen and possibly not" would be on an entirely different plane.

This is partly why one would be reluctant to say: "These people rigorously hold the opinion (or view) that there is a Last Judgement". "Opinion" sounds queer.

It is for this reason that different words are used: 'dogma', 'faith'.

We don't talk about hypothesis, or about high probability. Nor about knowing.

In a religious discourse we use such expressions as: "I believe that so and so will happen," and use them differently to the way in which we use them in science.

Although, there is a great temptation to think we do. Because we do talk of evidence, and do talk of evidence by experience.

We could even talk of historic events.

It has been said that Christianity rests on an historic basis.

It has been said a thousand times by intelligent people that indubitability is not enough in this case. Even if there is as much evidence as for Napoleon. Because the indubitability wouldn't be enough to make me change my whole life.

It doesn't rest on an historic basis in the sense that the ordinary belief in historic facts could serve as a foundation.

Here we have a belief in historic facts different from a belief in ordinary historic facts. Even, they are not treated as historical, empirical, propositions.

Those people who had faith didn't apply the doubt which would ordinarily apply to *any* historical propositions. Especially propositions of a time long past, etc.

What is the criterion of reliability, dependability? Suppose you give a general description as to when you say a proposition has a reasonable weight of probability. When you call it reasonable, is this *only* to say that for it you have such and such evidence, and for others you haven't?

For instance, we don't trust the account given of an event by a drunk man.

Father O'Hara[1] is one of those people who make it a question of science.

Here we have people who treat this evidence in a different way. They base things on evidence which taken in one way would

[1] Contribution to a Symposium on *Science and Religion* (Lond: Gerald Howe, 1931, pp. 107–116).

seem exceedingly flimsy. They base enormous things on this evidence. Am I to say they are unreasonable? I wouldn't call them unreasonable.

I would say, they are certainly not *reasonable*, that's obvious.

'Unreasonable' implies, with everyone, rebuke.

I want to say: they don't treat this as a matter of reasonability.

Anyone who reads the Epistles will find it said: not only that it is not reasonable, but that it is folly.

Not only is it not reasonable, but it doesn't pretend to be.

What seems to me ludicrous about O'Hara is his making it appear to be *reasonable*.

Why shouldn't one form of life culminate in an utterance of belief in a Last Judgement? But I couldn't either say "Yes" or "No" to the statement that there will be such a thing. Nor "Perhaps," nor "I'm not sure."

It is a statement which may not allow of any such answer.

If Mr. Lewy is religious and says he believes in a Judgement Day, I won't even know whether to say I understand him or not. I've read the same things as he's read. In a most important sense, I know what he means.

If an atheist says: "There won't be a Judgment Day, and another person says there will," do they mean the same?—Not clear what criterion of meaning the same is. They might describe the same things. You might say, this already shows that they mean the same.

We come to an island and we find beliefs there, and certain beliefs we are inclined to call religious. What I'm driving at is, that religious beliefs will not . . . They have sentences, and there are also religious statements.

These statements would not just differ in respect to what they are about. Entirely different connections would make them into religious beliefs, and there can easily be imagined transitions where we wouldn't know for our life whether to call them religious beliefs or scientific beliefs.

You may say they reason wrongly.

In certain cases you would say they reason wrongly, meaning they contradict us. In other cases you would say they don't reason at all, or "It is an entirely different kind of reasoning." The first, you would say in the case in which they reason in a similar way to us, and make something corresponding to our blunders.

Whether a thing is a blunder or not—it is a blunder in a particular system. Just as something is a blunder in a particular game and not in another.

You could also say that where we are reasonable, they are not reasonable—meaning they don't use *reason* here.

If they do something very like one of our blunders, I would say, I don't know. It depends on further surroundings of it.

It is difficult to see, in cases in which it has all the appearances of trying to be reasonable.

I would definitely call O'Hara unreasonable. I would say, if this is religious belief, then it's all superstition.

But I would ridicule it, not by saying it is based on insufficient evidence. I would say: here is a man who is cheating himself. You can say: this man is ridiculous because he believes, and bases it on weak reasons.

II

The word 'God' is amongst the earliest learnt—pictures and catechisms, etc. But not the same consequences as with pictures of aunts. I wasn't shown [that which the picture pictured].

The word is used like a word representing a person. God sees, rewards, etc.

"Being shown all these things, did you understand what this word meant?" I'd say: "Yes and no. I did learn what it didn't mean. I made myself understand. I could answer questions, understand questions when they were put in different ways—and in that sense could be said to understand."

If the question arises as to the existence of a god or God, it plays an entirely different role to that of the existence of any person or object I ever heard of. One said, had to say, that one *believed* in the existence, and if one did not believe, this was regarded as something bad. Normally if I did not believe in the existence of something no one would think there was anything wrong in this.

Also, there is this extraordinary use of the word 'believe'. One talks of believing and at the same time one doesn't use 'believe' as one does ordinarily. You might say (in the normal use): "You only believe—oh well. . . ." Here it is used entirely differently; on the other hand it is not used as we generally use the word 'know'.

If I even vaguely remember what I was taught about God, I might say: "Whatever believing in God may be, it can't be believing in something we can test, or find means of testing." You might say: "This is nonsense, because people say they believe on *evidence* or say they believe on religious experiences." I would say: "The mere fact that someone says they believe on evidence doesn't tell me enough for me to be able to say now whether I can say of a sentence 'God exists' that your evidence is unsatisfactory or insufficient."

Suppose I know someone, Smith. I've heard that he has been killed in a battle in this war. One day you come to me and say: "Smith is in Cambridge." I inquire, and find you stood at Guildhall and saw at the other end a man and said: "That was Smith." I'd say: "Listen. This isn't sufficient evidence." If we had a fair amount of evidence he was killed I would try to make you say that you're being credulous. Suppose he was never heard of again. Needless to say, it is quite impossible to make inquiries: "Who at 12.05 passed Market Place into Rose Crescent?" Suppose you say: "He was there". I would be extremely puzzled.

Suppose there is a feast on Mid-Summer Common. A lot of people stand in a ring. Suppose this is done every year and then everyone says he has seen one of his dead relatives on the other side of the ring. In this case, we could ask everyone in the ring. "Who did you hold by the hand?" Nevertheless, we'd all say that on that day we see our dead relatives. You could in this case say: "I had an extraordinary experience. I had the experience I can express by saying: 'I saw my dead cousin'." Would we say you are saying this on insufficient evidence? Under certain circumstances I would say this, under other circumstances I wouldn't. Where what is said sounds a bit absurd I would say: "Yes, in this case insufficient evidence." If altogether absurd, then I wouldn't.

Suppose I went to somewhere like Lourdes in France. Suppose I went with a very credulous person. There we see blood coming out of something. He says: "There you are, Wittgenstein, how can you doubt?" I'd say: "Can it only be explained one way?

Can't it be this or that?" I'd try to convince him that he'd seen nothing of any consequence. I wonder whether I would do that under all circumstances. I certainly know that I would under normal circumstances.

"Oughtn't one after all to consider this?" I'd say: "Come on. Come on." I would treat the phenomenon in this case just as I would treat an experiment in a laboratory which I thought badly executed.

"The balance moves when I will it to move." I point out it is not covered up, a draught can move it, etc.

I could imagine that someone showed an extremely passionate belief in such a phenomenon, and I couldn't approach his belief at all by saying: "This could just as well have been brought about by so and so" because he could think this blasphemy on my side. Or he might say: "It is possible that these priests cheat, but nevertheless in a different sense a miraculous phenomenon takes place there."

I have a statue which bleeds on such and such a day in the year. I have red ink, etc. "You are a cheat, but nevertheless the Deity uses you. Red ink in a sense, but not red ink in a sense."

Cf. Flowers at seance with label. People said: "Yes, flowers are materialized with label." What kind of circumstances must there be to make this kind of story not ridiculous?

I have a moderate education, as all of you have, and therefore know what is meant by insufficient evidence for a forecast. Suppose someone dreamt of the Last Judgement, and said he now knew what it would be like. Suppose someone said: "This is poor evidence." I would say: "If you want to compare it with the evidence for it's raining to-morrow it is no evidence at all." He may make it sound as if by stretching the point you may call it evidence. But it may be more than ridiculous as evidence. But now, would I be prepared to say: "You are basing your belief on extremely slender evidence, to put it mildly." Why should I regard this dream as evidence—measuring its validity as though I were measuring the validity of the evidence for meteorological events?

If you compare it with anything in Science which we call evidence, you can't credit that anyone could soberly argue: "Well, I had this dream . . . therefore . . . Last Judgement". You might say: "For a blunder, that's too big." If you suddenly wrote numbers down on the blackboard, and then said: "Now, I'm going to add," and then said: "2 and 21 is 13," etc. I'd say: "This is no blunder."

There are cases where I'd say he's mad, or he's making fun. Then there might be cases where I look for an entirely different interpretation altogether. In order to see what the explanation is I should have to see the sum, to see in what way it is done, what he makes follow from it, what are the different circumstances under which he does it, etc.

I mean, if a man said to me after a dream that he believed in the Last Judgement, I'd try to find what sort of impression it gave him. One attitude: "It will be in about 2,000 years. It will be bad for so and so and so, etc." Or it may be one of terror. In the case where there is hope, terror, etc., would I say there is insufficient evidence if he says: "I believe . . ."? I can't treat these words as I normally treat 'I believe so and so'. It would be entirely beside the point, and also if he said his friend so and so and his grandfather had had the dream and believed, it would be entirely beside the point.

I would not say: "If a man said he dreamt it would happen to-morrow," would he take his coat?, etc.

Case where Lewy has visions of his dead friend. Cases where you don't try to locate him. And case where you try to locate him in a business-like way. Another case where I'd say: "We can pre-suppose we have a broad basis on which we agree."

In general, if you say: "He is dead" and I say: "He is not dead" no-one would say: "Do they mean the same thing by 'dead'?" In the case where a man has visions I wouldn't offhand say: "He means something different."

Cf. A person having persecution mania.

What is the criterion for meaning something different? Not only what he takes as evidence for it, but also how he reacts, that he is in terror, etc.

How am I to find out whether this proposition is to be regarded as an empirical proposition—'You'll see your dead friend again?' Would I say: "He is a bit superstitious?" Not a bit.

He might have been apologetic. (The man who stated it

categorically was more intelligent than the man who was apologetic about it).

'Seeing a dead friend,' again means nothing much to me at all. I don't think in these terms. I don't say to myself: "I shall see so and so again" ever.

He always says it, but he doesn't make any search. He puts on a queer smile. "His story had that dreamlike quality." My answer would be in this case "Yes," and a particular explanation.

Take "God created man'. Pictures of Michelangelo showing the creation of the world. In general, there is nothing which explains the meanings of words as well as a picture, and I take it that Michelangelo was as good as anyone can be and did his best, and here is the picture of the Deity creating Adam.

If we ever saw this, we certainly wouldn't think this the Deity. The picture has to be used in an entirely different way if we are to call the man in that queer blanket 'God', and so on. You could imagine that religion was taught by means of these pictures. "Of course, we can only express ourselves by means of picture." This is rather queer . . . I could show Moore the pictures of a tropical plant. There is a technique of comparison between picture and plant. If I showed him the picture of Michelangelo and said: "Of course, I can't show you the real thing, only the picture" . . . . The absurdity is, I've never taught him the technique of using this picture.

It is quite clear that the role of pictures of Biblical subjects and rôle of the picture of God creating Adam are totally different ones. You might ask this question: "Did Michelangelo think that Noah in the ark looked like this, and that God creating Adam looked like this?" He wouldn't have said that God or Adam looked as they look in this picture.

It might seem as though, if we asked such a question as: "Does Lewy *really* mean what so and so means when he says so and so is alive?"—it might seem as though there were two sharply divided cases, one in which he would say he didn't mean it literally. I want to say this it not so. There will be cases where we will differ, and where it won't be a question at all of more or less knowledge, so that we can come together. Sometimes it will be a question of experience, so you can say: "Wait another 10 years." And I would say: "I would disencourage this kind of reasoning" and Moore would say: "I wouldn't disencourage it." That is, one would *do* something. We would take sides, and that goes so far that there would really be great differences between us, which might come out in Mr. Lewy saying: "Wittgenstein is trying to undermine reason", and this wouldn't be false. This is actually where such questions rise.

III

Today I saw a poster saying: " 'Dead' Undergraduate speaks."

The inverted commas mean: "He isn't really dead." "He isn't what people call dead. They call it 'dead' not quite correctly."

We don't speak of "door" in quotes.

It suddenly struck me: "If someone said 'He isn't really dead, although by the ordinary criteria he is dead'—couldn't I say "He is not only dead by the ordinary criteria;he is what we all call 'dead'."

If you now call him 'alive', you're using language in a queer way, because you're almost deliberately preparing misunderstandings. Why don't you use some other word, and let "dead" have the meaning it already has?

Suppose someone said: "It didn't always have this meaning. He's not dead according to the old meaning" or "He's not dead according to the old idea".

What is it, to have different ideas of death? Suppose you say: "I have the idea of myself being a chair after death" or "I have the idea of myself being a chair in half-an-hour"—you all know under what circumstances we say of something that it has become a chair.

C.f. (1) "This shadow will cease to exist."

(2) "This chair will cease to exist." You say that you know what this chair ceasing to exist is like. But you have to think. You may find that there isn't a use for this sentence. You think of the use.

I imagine myself on the death-bed. I imagine you all looking at the air above me. You say "You have an idea".

Are you clear when you'd say you had ceased to exist?

You have six different ideas [of 'ceasing to exist'] at different times.

If you say: "I can imagine myself being a disembodied spirit. Wittgenstein, can you imagine yourself as a disembodied spirit?" —I'd say: "I'm sorry. I [so far] connect nothing with these words."

I connect all sorts of complicated things with these words. I think of what people have said of sufferings after death, etc.

"I have two different ideas, one of ceasing to exist after death, the other of being a disembodied spirit."

What's it like to have two different ideas? What is the criterion for one man having one idea, another man having another idea?

You gave me two phrases, "ceasing to exist", "being a disembodied spirit". "When I say this, I think of myself having a certain set of experiences." What is it like to think of this?

If you think of your brother in America, how do you know that what you think is, that the thought inside you is, of your brother being in America? Is this an experiential business?

Cf. How do you know that what you want is an apple? [Russell].

How do you know that you believe that your brother is in America?

A pear might be what satisfied you. But you wouldn't say: "What I wanted was an apple."

Suppose we say that the thought is some sort of process in his mind, or his saying something, etc.—then I could say: "All right, you call this a thought of your brother in America, well, what is the connection between this and your brother in America?"

Lewy: You might say that this is a question of convention.

Why is it that you don't doubt that it is a thought of your brother in America?

One process [the thought] seems to be a shadow or a picture of something else.

How do I know that a picture is a picture of Lewy?—Normally by its likeness to Lewy, or, under certain circumstances, a picture of Lewy may not be like him, but like Smith. If I give up the business of being like [as a criterion], I get into an awful mess, because anything may be his portrait, given a certain method of projection.

If you said that the thought was in some way a picture of his brother in America—Yes, but by what method of projection is it a picture of this? How queer it is that there should be no doubt what its a picture of.

If you're asked: "How do you know it is a thought of such and such?" the thought that immediately comes to your mind is one of a shadow, a picture. You don't think of a causal relation. The kind of relation you think of is best expressed by "picture", "shadow," etc.

The word "picture" is even quite all right—in many cases it is even in the most ordinary sense, a picture. You might translate my very words into a picture.

But the point is this, suppose you drew this, how do I know it is my brother in America? Who says it is him—unless it is here ordinary similarity?

What is the connection between these words, or anything substitutable for them, with my brother in America?

The first idea [you have] is that you are looking at your own thought, and are absolutely sure that it is a thought that so and so. You are looking at some mental phenomenon, and you say to yourself "obviously this is a thought of my brother being in America". It seems to be a super-picture. It seems, with thought, that there is no doubt whatever. With a picture, it still depends on the method of projection, whereas here it seems that you get rid of the projecting relation, and are absolutely certain that this is thought of that.

Smythies's muddle is based on the idea of a super—picture.

We once talked about how the idea of certain superlatives came about in Logic. The idea of a super-necessity, etc.

"How do I know that this is the thought of my brother in America?"—that *what* is the thought?

Suppose my thought consists of my *saying* "My brother is in America"—how do I know that I *say* my brother is in America?

How is the connection made?—We imagine at first a connection like strings.

Lewy: The connection is a convention. The word designates.

You must explain "designates" by examples. We have learnt a rule, a practice, etc.

Is thinking of something like painting or shooting at something?

It seems like a projection connection, which seems to make it indubitable, although there is not a projection relation at all.

If I said "My brother is in America"—I could imagine there being rays projecting from my words to my brother in America. But what if my brother isn't in America?—then the rays don't hit anything.

[If you say that the words refer to my brother by expressing the proposition that my brother is in America—the proposition being a middle link between the words and what they refer to] —What has the proposition, the mediate link, got to do with America?

The most important point is this—if you talk of painting, etc. your idea is that the connection exists *now*, so that it seem as though as long as I do this thinking, this connection exists.

Whereas, if we said it is a connection of convention, there would be no point in saying it exists while we think. There is a connection by convention—What do we mean?—This connection refers to events happening at various times. Most of all, it refers to a technique.

["Is thinking something going on at a particular time, or is it spread over the words?" "It comes in a flash." "Always?—it sometimes does come in a flash, although this may be all sorts of different things.]

If it does refer to a technique, then it can't be enough, in certain cases, to explain what you mean in a few words; because there is something which might be thought to be in conflict with the idea going on from 7 to 7.5, namely the practice of using it [the phrase.]

When we talked of: "So and so is an automaton", the strong hold of that view was [due to the idea] that you could say: "Well, I know what I mean" . . . , as though you were looking at something happening while you said the thing, entirely independant of what came before and after, the application [of the phrase]. It looked as though you could talk of understanding a word, without any reference to the technique of its usage. It looked as though Smythies said he could understand the sentence, and that we then had nothing to say.

What was it like to have different ideas of death?—What I meant was—Is having an idea of death something like having a certain picture, so that you can say "I have an idea of death from 5 to 5.1 etc."? "In whatever way anyone will use this word, I have now a certain idea"—if you call this "having an idea", then it is not what is commonly called "having an idea", because what is commonly called "having an idea", has a reference to the technique of the word, etc.

We are all here using the word "death", which is a public

instrument, which has a whole technique [of usage]. Then someone says he has an idea of death. Something queer; because you might say "You are using the word 'death', which is an instrument functioning in a certain way."

If you treat this [your idea] as something private, with what right are you calling it an idea of death?—I say this, because we, also, have a right to say what is an idea of death.

He might say "I have my own private idea of death"—why call this an 'idea of death' unless it is something you connect with death. Although this [your 'idea'] might not interest us at all. [In this case,] it does not belong on the game played with 'death', which we all know and understand.

If what he calls his "idea of death" is to become relevant, it must become part of our game.

'My idea of death is the separation of the soul from the body' —if we know what to do with these words. He can also say: "I connect with the word 'death' a certain picture—a woman lying in her bed"—that may or may not be of some interest.

If he connects

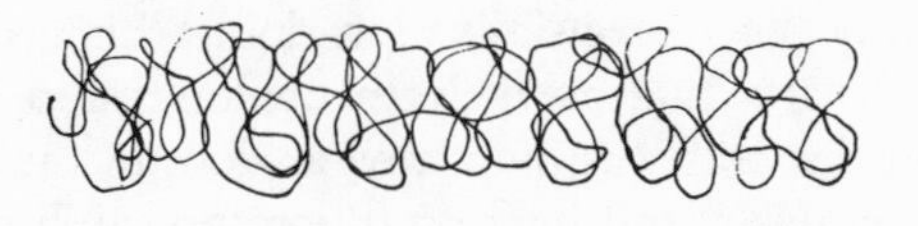

with death, and this was his idea, this might be interesting psychologically.

"The separation of soul from body" [only had a public interest.] This may act like black curtains or it may not act like black curtains. I'd have to find out what the consequences [of your saying it] are. I am not, at least, at present at all clear. [You say this]—"So what?"—I know these words, I have certain pictures. All sorts of things go along with these words.

If he says this, I won't know yet what consequences he will draw. I don't know what he opposes this to.

Lewy: "You oppose it to being extinguished."

If you say to me—"Do you cease to exist?"—I should be bewildered, and would not know what exactly this is to mean.

"If you dont cease to exist, you will suffer after death", there I begin to attach ideas, perhaps ethical ideas of responsibility. The point is, that although these are well-known words, and although I can go from one sentence to another sentence, or to pictures [I don't know what consequences you draw from this statement].

Suppose someone said: "What do you believe, Wittgenstein? Are you a sceptic? Do you know whether you will survive death?" I would really, this is a fact, say "I can't say. I don't know", because I haven't any clear idea what I'm saying when I'm saying "I don't cease to exist," etc.

Spiritualists make one kind of connection.

A Spiritualist says "Apparition" etc. Although he gives me a picture I don't like, I do get a clear idea. I know that much, that some people connect this phrase with a particular kind of verification. I know that some people don't—religious people e.g.—they don't refer to a verification, but have entirely different ideas.

A great writer said that, when he was a boy, his father set him a task, and he suddenly felt that nothing, not even death, could take away the responsibility [in doing this task]; this was his duty to do, and that even death couldn't stop it being his duty. He said that this was, in a way, a proof of the immortality of the soul—because if this lives on [the responsibility won't die.] The idea is given by what we call the proof. Well, if this is the idea, [all right].

If a Spiritualist wishes to give *me* an idea of what he means or doesn't mean by 'survival', he can say all sorts of things—

[If I ask what idea he has, I may be given what the Spiritualists say or I may be given what the man I quoted said, etc., etc.]

I would at least [in the case of the Spiritualist] have an idea of what this sentence is connected up with, and get more and more of an idea as I see what he does with it.

As it is, I hardly connect anything with it at all.

Suppose someone, before going to China, when he might never see me again, said to me: "We might see one another after death"—would I necessarily say that I don't understand him? I might say [want to say] simply, "Yes. I *understand* him entirely."

Lewy "In this case, you might only mean that he expressed a certain attitude."

I would say "No, it isn't the same as saying 'I'm very fond of you' "—and it may not be the same as saying anything else. It says what it says. Why should you be able to substitute anything else?

Suppose I say: "The man used a picture."

"Perhaps now he sees he was wrong." What sort of remark is this?

"God's eye sees everything"—I want to say of this that it uses a picture.

I don't want to belittle him [the person who says it.]

Suppose I said to him "You've been using a picture", and he said "No, this is not all"—mightn't he have misunderstood me? What do I want to do [by saying this]? What would be the real sign of disagreement? What might be the real criterion of his disagreeing with me?

Lewy: "If he said: 'I've been making preparations [for death]."

Yes, this might be a disagreement—if he himself were to use the word in a way in which I did not expect, or were to draw conclusions I did not expect him to draw. I wanted only to draw attention to a particular technique of usage. We should disagree, if he was using a technique I didn't expect.

We associate a particular use with a picture.

Smythies: 'This isn't all he does—associate a use with a picture.'

Wittgenstein: Rubbish. I meant: what conclusions are you going to draw? etc. Are eyebrows going to be talked of, in connection with the Eye of God?

"He could just as well have said so and so"—this [remark] is foreshadowed by the word "attitude". He couldn't just as well have said something else.

If I say he used a picture, I don't want to say anything he himself wouldn't say. I want to say that he draws these conclusions.

Isn't it as important as anything else, what picture he does use?

Of certain pictures we say that they might just as well be replaced by another—e.g. we could, under certain circumstances, have one projection of an ellipse drawn instead of another.

[He *may* say]: "I would have been prepared to use another picture, it would have had the same effect. . . ."

The whole *weight* may be in the picture.

We can say in chess that the exact shape of the chess-men plays no rôle. Suppose that the main pleasure was, to see people ride; then, playing it in writing wouldn't be playing the same game. Someone might say: "All he's done is change the shape of the head"—what more could he do?

When I say he's using a picture I'm merely making a *grammatical* remark: [What I say] can only be verified by the consequences he does or does not draw.

If Smythies disagrees, I don't take notice of this disagreement.

All I wished to characterize was the conventions he wished to draw. If I wished to say anything more I was merely being philosophically arrogant.

Normally, if you say "He is an automaton " you draw consequences, if you stab him, [he'll feel pain]. On the other hand, you may not wish to draw any such consequences, and this is all there is to it—except further muddles.

Made in the USA
Lexington, KY
03 December 2016

Amish Weddings

The Widower's Baby

Book Two

Samantha Bayarr

This novel is a work of fiction. Names, characters, and incidents are the product of the author's imagination, and are therefore used fictitiously. Any similarity or resemblance to actual persons; living or dead, places or events is purely coincidental and beyond the intent of the author or publisher.

All brand names or product names mentioned in this book are the sole ownership of their respective holders. Livingston Hall Publishers is not associated with any products or brands named in this book

A note from the Author:

While this novel is set against the backdrop of an Amish community, the characters and the names of the community are fictional. There is no intended resemblance between the characters in this book or the setting, and any real members of any Amish or Mennonite community. As with any work of fiction, I've taken license in some areas of research as a means of creating the necessary circumstances for my characters and setting. It is completely impossible to be accurate in details and descriptions, since every community differs, and such a setting would destroy the fictional quality of entertainment this book serves to present. Any inaccuracies in the Amish and Mennonite lifestyles portrayed in this book are completely due to fictional license. Please keep in mind that this book is meant for fictional, entertainment purposes only, and is not written as a text book on the Amish.

Happy Reading

If you have not read Book ONE in this series, this book will not make much sense, as it is a continuing series that incorporates all the characters from each book. Click HERE to get a copy of Ellie's Homecoming.

Chapter 1

Lydia's tormented screams reached Eli all the way to the barn, filling him with a fear he'd never known before. Hannah had urged him to call for the doctor, explaining it was too much of a gamble for a midwife alone.

Was she as fearful as he was?

His beautiful wife had tried to insist she didn't need or want the doctor, but Eli had gone against her wishes, worry forcing a decision out of him.

Desperation motivated him as he dialed the number with a shaky hand. He'd had the phone

installed in the barn for this exact kind of emergency, and he prayed now that the doctor would answer.

He paced impatiently on the floor of the barn, crushing the fresh hay beneath his feet, while he waited through four rings. When the voicemail began, he hung up, saying another hasty prayer asking for guidance.

Hannah had used the term *breech,* and he'd lost a foal recently for the same reason, and he was terrified of the same fate for his child.

Another chilling scream rent the air, startling him out of the stupor of his prayer. He focused on the phone and dialed the emergency line, begging for an ambulance with one long, ragged breath. Tears pooled in his eyes as he answered several questions that indicated the person on the other end of the line was just as afraid for the safety of his wife and child.

"Please hurry," Eli pleaded with the man. "I have to get back to *mei fraa.* She needs me."

He set the phone down, the man still trying to get him to answer, but Eli was not thinking straight. Stumbling back to the house, he pleaded with God to save his family, each heavy step bringing more anxiety as he made his way back to them.

Once inside, Lydia's screams made him cringe, but there was something different about them now. As he made his way up the stairs to their room, he realized they had become weak and faint.

Forcing his feet to take him to her bedside, he avoided the scene at the foot of the bed where Hannah mopped up blood from the sheets. The sight of it made his heart race, but he wouldn't let either of them know how terrified he was.

He collapsed onto his knees and buried his face in his wife's neck, kissing her and whispering in her ear.

"I'm here, Lydia. Be strong."

She let out another weak cry, and then he heard the squeal from his child. He looked back at the infant, feeling his wife's grip on his hand loosen.

He watched with unseeing eyes as Hannah placed the *boppli* in Lydia's waiting arms, her smile weak, but proud.

"She has your blue eyes," Lydia whispered to her husband. "And blond, curly hair like her *mamm.*"

Eli watched his wife coo to her new daughter, and look up into his eyes. Her eyes were cloudy and dull, and her face seemed weighted down with a sadness.

"I want *mei dochder* to have a *mamm,"* she said with great effort.

"She has a *mamm,* Lydia. She has you." He didn't like the labored sound of her voice, nor did he like the words she was speaking.

"Nee, I don't think I'm going to make it."

"Shh," he begged his wife, his lower lip quivering. "Please don't talk like that. I called an ambulance, and they're going to take you to the hospital, and everything is going to be just fine, ain't so, Hannah?"

He looked up at the young woman who was working desperately and frantically mopping up blood his wife was losing. She glanced at him only for a flicker of a moment, and then nodded as she focused her attention back to the emergency that his wife's condition presented.

Lydia kissed the baby's face and smiled.

"Name her Mira, after *mei mamm,"* she said, and then motioned weakly for Hannah to come nearer.

She reluctantly left her task, knowing it wasn't making much difference.

"Hannah," Lydia whispered. "I want you to be her *mamm."*

"Nee, you're her *mamm,* Lydia," she said, forcing a smile around the tears in her eyes.

"You're going to be chasing after her for many years to come."

She placed a hand on Lydia's arm, and then went back to the task of cleaning, but she knew if the ambulance didn't hurry, they were going to lose her.

Eli held her close, rocking her back and forth, willing her to live, but it was all in vain, and his heart sank at the reality. *"Gott,* please!" he whispered into her hair.

In the distance, he could hear the faint sound of sirens from the nearing ambulance.

Lydia smiled at her husband. "Promise me you'll marry Hannah so our *dochder* will have a *mamm."*

He hesitated, not wanting to commit to such a foolish thing.

"Promise me," she said weakly.

"I promise," he whispered, glancing briefly at Hannah, hoping she hadn't heard his promise, but she had.

Lydia exhaled weakly, and didn't draw another breath. He pulled her away from him and jostled her.

"*Gott,* please don't take her from me," he sobbed.

He could hear the ambulance pulling into the driveway of their home, but Eli knew it was too late. She'd already drawn her last breath, and there would not be another.

Chapter 2

Eli watched methodically as Hannah wept quietly while she prepared Lydia's body to be taken by the mortician, where she would be further prepared for burial, and then brought back for the funeral.

Nothing seemed real to him anymore.

His sister and *mamm* had gathered in the corner of the room quietly to watch the doctor check over his child.

He could hear her crying, but he couldn't go to her.

His *boppli.*

He hadn't even really looked at her, except when Lydia had pointed out the blond curls that matched her own.

It didn't matter now. The child belonged to Hannah. His wife had given her the child, and he would honor her wishes. He didn't know what to do with the child. He wasn't her *mamm,* and he had no idea how to be. A girl would need a woman's care more than she would need him, and he hadn't even been able to bring himself to looking at her a second time. He feared it would cause him to break down if he saw too much of his wife in the child.

Ellie stood next to her twin brother, trying to urge him away from the morbid scene in front of him. He held fast to Lydia's hand, staring blankly, but unmovable. She had to wonder if he even heard her or knew she was there. She prayed silently that her brother's mourning would not consume him.

It wasn't that she didn't feel he had a right to grieve, but he had a new daughter who would need him to be strong. She felt sorry for Hannah, who had confided in her about Lydia's last moment before she passed on, knowing what a burden such a promise could be. She tried to reassure Hannah that everything would be alright in a day or so. They would get through the funeral, but she agreed Eli would need some help

with the *boppli.* Ellie had encouraged her to stay on for an extra week to help her brother with the transition. Not exactly knowing how to react to the dying wish of her sister-in-law, whom she barely knew, Ellie tried to assure Hannah that it would likely be forgotten in a few days.

Seeing her brother now, Ellie had to wonder if she believed that herself.

Eli's attention turned to Hannah as she cleaned the baby and wrapped her in a blanket. He could hear her soft breath as she presented the child to him. His arms would not reach out to her. He stared blankly at the bundle in front of him, but could not look at her face. Little gurgles and squeaks reverberated from the folds of the blankets, and the child seemed content where she was.

He shook his head, and put up a hand.

"*Nee,*" he said firmly, keeping his lower jaw clenched to keep it from quivering with sorrow. "She needs a *mamm.* You are her *mamm* now, Hannah."

Hannah's breath hitched. She pulled the infant close to her, feeling elation and sorrow swirling inside her. She'd overheard the promise Lydia had prompted from Eli, knowing he'd only accepted to appease his wife. Surely he didn't mean to give away his child. As much as she wanted to have a child of her own, she could not

accept such a burden, for Eli would take her back when he was finished grieving, and she would mourn the child forever.

Ellie hadn't missed the look on Hannah's face, and it caused her to worry. She knew the deep desire her friend had for wanting a baby of her own, and it wasn't right for her brother to dangle that over her head, no matter how much he was grieving.

She placed a hand on her brother's shoulder. "You don't mean that," she whispered. "She needs you. You're her *familye.*"

"Nee," he said angrily. "*Mei familye* is gone. *Mei fraa* is dead, and the *boppli* is Hannah's. She will have to raise her alone, because I'm not marrying her the way I promised Lydia."

Tears pooled in his eyes, and he fled from the room, leaving Hannah holding his child.

Chapter 3

Eli rose from the edge of the bed, having ignored the desperate knocks at the door from his sister, knowing it was time for the funeral.

Nothing could prepare him for this, and even his prayers were too weak to comfort him. He'd slept for the past two days, not thinking about his child. He'd overheard his *mamm* and sister telling Hannah they would return with a couple of bottles so she could give the infant goat's milk. After he'd snatched a few things from the room he no longer shared with Lydia, he'd taken them out to the *dawdi haus,* where he'd remained for the past two days. He hadn't wanted to face what was before him, and now, as

Ellie knocked at the door relentlessly, he would have to.

His tongue stuck to the roof of his mouth as he tried to tell her to leave him alone, but she continued to knock and call out to him. His head ached as he stumbled to the door and opened it just a crack, his eyes squinting against the bright morning sun that streamed in through the opening.

Ellie stood there, clad in a black mourning dress and bonnet.

He couldn't look at her.

She stared at her brother's disheveled clothing that he'd likely slept in for the past two days, his auburn hair standing on end on one side. She felt sorry for him, and wanted to pull him into her arms and make the pain go away, but she couldn't imagine being in his place. She could see the torment in his blank stare, his posture speaking volumes of his pain.

"Hannah and *Mira* are waiting in the buggy with *Mamm* and Jonas. We'll wait for you to dress."

She'd spoken his child's name so softly; he'd barely heard her.

He didn't want to hear it; he simply nodded and closed the door.

His thoughts slammed against his brain; he didn't want to think anymore. He was a father; it was what he and Lydia had wanted so much, and now she was gone trying to give that to him. His arms were empty, and his heart was broken beyond repair. How could he go and bury his wife the way his family expected him to? He knew the community would frown if he was not there, and he also knew they would frown if the child was not there, but he couldn't deal with her right now. He had to get through the funeral and the meal afterward that he would be expected to attend.

He felt as if someone had knocked the wind out of him, and he hadn't the strength or the will to draw in a breath.

Had his *mamm* felt this way when she'd buried his *daed?*

One would never have known; she'd handled herself with grace and a quiet dignity. He couldn't do that; he wasn't as strong as she was.

He combed through his hair and looked at himself in the mirror, tugging on the long whiskers along his jaw. He'd grown the beard as an outward sign he was married, but now he was not.

He no longer had a wife.

I should have no beard, he thought to himself as he stared at his reflection.

Picking up a pair of scissors, he pulled a section of his beard and began to cut away at it angrily. His throat constricted as he remembered all the times Lydia would rake her fingers through it when they would cuddle. But as he looked in the mirror, watching himself lop off his beard, he was compelled to erase all remembrance of her, hoping it would take away the hurt he felt deep in the pit of his stomach.

When he'd cut as much as he could, he picked up his razor and shaved his chin thoughtfully, every stroke of the blade just as intentional as the one before it. He didn't stop until his chin was smooth.

He could be shunned for such an act of rebellion, but he didn't care. If it would keep him from having to attend Lydia's …

He closed his eyes against the thought of her funeral. He wasn't ready to say goodbye or let her go.

He dressed and shuffled his feet toward the door, wishing he didn't have to go through with this.

If he could bury his head in his pillow until the pain left him, he would. Sleep was the only way to keep his mind quiet of the thoughts that hurt so deeply.

Opening the door, he didn't expect Ellie to still be standing there waiting on him. She drew a hand to her mouth to stifle the gasp, but the look in her eyes spoke volumes of her shock at seeing his clean-shaven face.

"Not a word," he grumbled under his breath as he made his way to the waiting buggy.

His mother shared his sister's reaction, but she didn't say a word as he climbed in the open seat next to his brother-in-law. When they neared the graveyard, Eli choked up at seeing the entire community of buggies lined along the road. They had all gathered to pay their respects the same way they had when his father had passed on. His mother put a hand on his shoulder from behind him, but he was too inconsolable for it to comfort him.

Hannah felt awkward holding his child in his presence. He'd glanced at her briefly before climbing into the buggy, and she wondered if it was intentional. Had he wanted her to notice his clean-shaven face? She tried not to read too much into it, but had to wonder if he intended to follow through with the promise he'd made to Lydia. His mother had asked her to stay and care for the infant, and she'd agreed only for the child's sake. He was in no shape to take care of her, and from the way he reacted to her just now, it might be a

permanent situation with her, and she would accept that.

In the two days that she'd cared for Mira, she admittedly had grown attached to her, despite every effort to guard her heart. She knew that if Eli didn't take over the care of his child soon, it would only be that much more difficult for her to separate herself from little Mira if he refused to honor his promise. Being the closest thing she'd likely ever get to having a *boppli* of her own, she considered offering to stay on as nanny to the child if that was all he would offer, and despite how tough it would be if she had to let go, she'd prayed for God's will.

Jonas parked the buggy, and hopped down to help the women out. Eli stared at the ground, allowing Ellie to take hold of Mira so Hannah could get out. She extended the child toward her brother, but he shook his head, his mouth forming a deep frown as he continued to keep his eyes cast down.

She sighed heavily, showing disapproval of her brother's reaction, but decided to let it go for now. Rather than say something she might regret, she prayed he'd bond with the child before she became too attached to Hannah, and she to the child.

She handed the baby back to Hannah, and urged her to walk beside her brother. It was

proper for him to have his child at his side during the service, but she wasn't so sure about Hannah's presence—especially given her brother's clean-shaven face. She imagined the Bishop would take that as a sign he was willing to accept Hannah as a wife, and would likely expect him to marry her. Still, he should have waited to shave until a respectable amount of time had passed.

It was too late for all of that now.

Chapter 4

"I think you should marry Hannah the way you promised Lydia."

The Bishop's statement was more than mere suggestion, and Eli knew it.

The *only* reason he would even consider such a thing would be to make sure she continued to take care of the child. She would have to understand that he would never be a husband to her, but he doubted she would ever agree to it.

He would ask her just the same.

He knew the Bishop would not accept her continuing to live on his property without a marriage between them, even though he would stay in the *dawdi haus,* but he needed her to take

care of the *boppli.* She would be nothing more to him than a nanny, and someone to cook for him and wash his clothes.

He put down the plate of food he had no intention of eating now. He couldn't believe he was even entertaining such thoughts when he'd just put his wife to rest less than an hour ago, but he had no other option if he wanted Hannah to stay on to take care of the child.

How could he honor such a promise when his heart would never be in it. He and Hannah had a history, and she'd want a regular marriage. As his friend, she deserved nothing less than that, but he wasn't the one to give her that.

The Bishop had strictly warned him they would have to be married immediately, or she would have to leave his home. Could he let her take the child—Lydia's child?

No; that was out of the question.

But so was a marriage for anything other than convenience. He would never betray Lydia's place in his heart by opening up to another woman in her stead, and he could never be anything more than friends with Hannah.

He glanced at her from the other side of the living-room of the Hochstetler's home where they'd gathered for the post-funeral meal. They weren't Lydia's family, but they were the closest

thing she had to a real family; she'd come to stay with the older couple when she'd moved to the community. *Frau* Hochstetler had been friends with Lydia's *mamm,* and so when the woman passed away, she'd moved here with them. It had been Eli's luck, or so he thought.

Now, all he could think about was wishing he'd never met her so he wouldn't have to endure the pain of losing her. Was it right to wish for such a selfish thing? His jaw clenched as he looked away from the woman, who was not his wife, holding his child. He was supposed to share that child with the love of his life. Now all he felt was empty and broken. His faith was weak, and his heart ached with a deep sadness he hadn't even felt when his own father had passed away.

Though he knew he was obligated to marry Hannah, he felt nothing short of pure terror at the thought of it.

"I'll make all the arrangements," the Bishop was saying.

What? Had he missed an entire conversation just now?

He looked at Bishop Troyer blankly.

"I'm sure the Hochstetler's will be more than happy to accommodate the wedding. They cared for Lydia a great deal, and would want to make certain you and her *boppli* were well-cared

for. Hannah will make an excellent *fraa.* In time, you'll heal, and be able to love her."

Eli put a hand to his mouth to cover the bile he thought was sure would escape him if he didn't stifle it.

Breathe, just breathe, he said to himself.

"My suggestion is that we *handle* it before the end of the week," he continued, despite Eli's apparent aversion to the subject. "Any longer than that and you'll have to either move from your farm, or move her off the property. It won't be considered proper after that, except that we know you're staying in the *dawdi haus."*

How? Did either Ellie or Hannah tell you my business?

Either way, he wasn't ready to think about getting married in front of the entire community. He'd just buried his wife, and already the Bishop was deciding and planning for his future wedding. He knew it was the way of the *Ordnung,* but that didn't mean he had to accept it, did it?

He supposed it did if he intended to remain in the community.

The real question weighing on his mind was; did he want to remain in the community?

He supposed he did if he wanted to have a mother for the child Lydia had left behind.

Chapter 5

Eli felt numb as he tried to react appropriately as the entire community either hugged him or shook his hand, offering condolences and raving about what a beautiful gift Lydia had left behind in Mira.

Guilt tugged at his heart every time a comment was made about the child. He hadn't set eyes on her since the moment she was born. He'd been too preoccupied with Lydia's passing to notice too much about the infant, but he had heard her all day at the funeral. She'd cried and cooed, and slept soundly, though he was very aware of her soft breathing even from across the room.

Was that his only connection to her? Lydia would likely have called it intuition, but to him, it only served as a grim reminder of his loss.

He knew what was expected of him, and he wasn't sure if he could go through with it.

When everyone had left, his *mamm* approached him and pulled him into an awkward hug. He feared really hugging her back because he knew it would cause him to breakdown, and he wasn't ready to face the emotions that had plagued him since his *fraa* had taken her last breath.

"I know this is a difficult time for you," she said quietly. "But you need to think of the *boppli* now. She's not Hannah's responsibility—unless you do what's right and marry her. I understand your reluctance to bond with Mira, because I imagine she reminds you too much of Lydia, but that's not fair to the wee one."

She knew him well; he couldn't deny that.

He wanted to collapse in her arms and cry like a child, but he clenched his jaw instead, stifling his emotions that begged to be let loose. It tortured him, despite his attempts to get past his obligations. He longed for the end of the day when he could collapse onto the bed in the *dawdi haus* when he could sleep away his grief.

"Do you want me to talk to her for you?" his *mamm* asked.

"I can't be a husband to her the way she deserves," he confessed, feeling a large weight lift from him.

"I know," she whispered. "You can't do it on your own, but *Gott* will help you."

"I *can't,"* he said weakly.

"Each day will get easier. You and I have something in common now, and I understand your heart is breaking. I had the luxury of being able to grieve, but you have to think of Lydia's *boppli: your boppli.* She loved that *boppli,* and that was her gift she left behind for you. When the breaking in your heart begins to lift, you'll be able to hold her and protect her the way your *fraa* made you promise. You *must* do this for her; it was her last wish for you and her *kinner."*

He understood what his *mamm* was trying to say; it made sense to him, but his heart would not cooperate. He could feel the emotion rising up in him, trying to escape. The tears filled his eyes and his throat constricted, his breath hitched and he clenched his jaw to stop it, but it was too late. Tears poured from his eyes despite every attempt to stifle them. He evened out his breathing trying his best to keep the others in the room from knowing what they could not see with his back turned to them. His mother had a way about her

that continued to bring it out. She wept as she held him close, and he was comforted by her sobs that covered up his own sorrowful tears that continued to spill uncontrollably.

For some minutes, he wept alongside his mother, letting her embrace beget more tears from him than he ever thought he had in him. Before he could break free, Ellie had covered the two of them with her arms, and soon Jonas was among them, praying quietly. Bishop Troyer laid his hands on them and prayed, while he encouraged Hannah to join them, but she shook her head and cast her eyes to the ground.

She would wait for Eli to come to her on his own terms, whatever they may be. She would not take advantage of his grief. She'd made that mistake once and it had almost cost her the friends that now stood by Eli's side comforting him. She didn't belong there—not yet anyway. Her turn would come, but today was not that day. Eli needed time to recover his loss, and she would wait on him and the Lord to make her decision. If Mira was to be her child, she would wait on the Lord for a sure sign.

Though she felt a prompting from the Lord to be patient and wait on him, she was tempted to bolt from the house. Her nerves had been spent, and her heart was near-breaking. Her faith made her stay; she would stay until God told her to go,

but she prayed faithfully that he would not make her. She loved Mira already, and she would love Eli if the Lord told her to do so, and she would marry him, even if it was only a marriage of convenience. She had been willing to marry Jonas for lesser reasons, but Eli and Mira were a whole different story. They needed her just as much as she needed them, and for that reason, she would wait. She would wait on God, and she would wait on Eli, no matter how long he asked her to.

Lord, speed his healing, and mend his heart. Give him a heart for his dochder, and for me, if it be your will. Bless me with the strength to wait until you give me your blessing, and the grace to accept if your answer is no.

Her prayer surprised her; she hadn't expected it, and when she opened her eyes, Eli was standing before her.

Had he heard her whisper of a prayer?

She waited for him to hold out his arms to his child, but he wouldn't even look at her tiny sleeping form resting her head on Hannah's shoulder.

"I'd like to talk to you in private," was all he said and then walked toward the front door.

Was she supposed to follow him?

Before she could make up her mind, Ellie was extending her arms to relieve her of the

boppli. Her throat tightened and she kissed the top of her head, breathing her in as if it was the last time she might hold her.

With shaky hands she turned over the child to Ellie and reluctantly went to meet Eli to discover the fate of her future.

Chapter 6

Eli pulled in a deep breath, and paced the width of the driveway while he waited for Hannah to join him. He had no idea what he was going to say to her, or how he would go about convincing her that his plan was to her benefit. He'd seen in her eyes how attached she was to his daughter, and he prayed that would be enough to convince her to accept his proposal on his terms. He knew that it wasn't fair to ask such a thing, and that it could destroy their friendship, but his only concern at the moment was to provide for the child by giving her a mother. He was not prepared to take care of the child, and he had no idea if he would ever develop a fatherly instinct for her the way that Lydia had hoped.

Guilt tugged at his heart, as he realized he was letting Lydia down. She had wanted a real family for her child, and that was why she'd made him promise to marry Hannah in the first place. He swallowed hard as he realized she'd walked up behind him and was waiting for him to speak his peace.

Right away, he noticed that she'd left the child inside the house with his family. He was grateful for that, knowing it would be easier on him if he didn't have to see her. He already felt guilty enough for not being the father that his wife had wanted him to be.

He looked Hannah in the eye, pausing as he searched for the right words; even though he had no idea what he was going to say to her, but at least he was able to concentrate better without the distraction of the child.

He opened his mouth to speak, but the words would not come. He didn't want to marry Hannah for too many reasons; the biggest of these being that he'd just buried his wife. But the truth of the matter was, Mira needed a mother, and he knew he was not up to the task. Was it right to use his child as a lure for a marriage of convenience? He knew Hannah's desire to have a child of her own, and he felt he was taking advantage of her, but having a chance to be a mother was all he could offer her.

Hannah shifted from one foot to the other, wondering if she should just let Eli off the hook. "I'd like to offer my services as a nanny," she began.

"Nee," he interrupted her. "The Bishop will not allow you to remain on my property overnight to care for the *boppli* unless…"

He couldn't finish the sentence.

"You don't have to marry me, Eli," she said gently. "I know this must be painful for you. I wish I could make this easy for you."

He cleared his throat, hoping it would steady his voice, but his stomach clenched, resisting the words he had to get out before he lost his nerve.

"There is a way. You can accept a marriage of *convenience* with me in order to be the *boppli's mamm."*

"Jah," she said softly. "I can do that."

It wasn't exactly what she wanted for her future, but she didn't dare delay her answer for fear he would change his mind. If it meant she would be a *mamm,* she would be content with what she could get. Having a marriage of convenience and a *boppli* was better than being a childless spinster.

"I value your friendship, Hannah, and so did *Lydia,"* he said with a catch to his voice. "I know how difficult this is for you, but I need you to understand I won't be able to be a *husband* to you, and I won't be able to give you any *kinner* of your own."

His words were final. It was a reality she'd faced when she stepped aside for Ellie to marry Jonas, and now she was faced with it once again. But this time was different; this time, the offer came with a *boppli* but no real husband attached to it. Could she really accept such a thing and be happy? She thought of how empty her arms already felt without little Mira in them, and decided it would have to do.

"I understand," she said softly.

"I'll continue to live in the *dawdi haus,"* he said. "You can move your things into the main bedroom so you'll be across the hall from the *boppli."*

He was going to let her stay in his bedroom? What if he changed his mind later and wanted to move back in his house? She supposed she could move into one of the other rooms in the house, but she didn't understand why he didn't want her to stay where she was, except that it was now Mira's room. He'd moved the cradle into that room between the queen-size bed and the full-size crib, making the room even more crowded, but

she supposed if he was moving her into the main bedroom—the room he'd shared with his wife, she would have plenty of room to put the cradle in there. Hannah didn't understand his reasoning for moving her, other than the fact he might not understand the immediate need to have the baby sleeping close in the cradle for the first couple of weeks. She wasn't about to argue with him or tell him how to handle his own home.

At this point, she felt blessed to have a home, a *boppli,* and a husband—even if in name only.

Chapter 7

Eli tried his best to be quiet as he packed up his bedroom to make it ready for Hannah. If it were up to him, he'd seal up the room and never deal with the memory of losing his wife here, but he knew that wasn't exactly being realistic. He didn't want to be in the room, and he didn't want to move Lydia's things, but they were of no use to her now, and seeing them would only be a reminder she was gone. He intended to pack them away quickly in the attic, and never see them again. He would be married in the morning to Hannah, and he would make her as comfortable as possible in his home. It was the least he could do for her, given the burden of a loveless marriage he had contracted with her.

She would never be his *bride,* only the caretaker for the child he could not be a father to.

He wasn't exactly sure what it was that made the situation so difficult, but he could only deal with one problem at a time, and that was to somehow get over his wife's death. Perhaps once his heart healed, there would be room for the child, but right now he didn't feel there was.

He'd prayed hard that first night; he'd prayed until he'd fallen asleep from sheer exhaustion, but he never felt the peace that he sought. Sadly, even now, he was not able to set his gaze upon the child, for fear he would break down. His heart ached, and his soul felt empty. He didn't think he would ever be the same again, and now he understood his own *mamm's* feelings of despair since his *daed's* death. She had tried to tell him that each day would get easier, and it wouldn't always be this way, but right at the moment he wasn't sure he believed that.

After haphazardly packing up everything he could get his hands on, and stuffing it into the cedar trunk he'd brought down from the attic, Eli thoughtfully lifted his wife's nightgown from the peg on the wall where she'd left it the night before she'd died. He drew it to his face, burying his nose in it, and breathing in her scent that still lingered on the garment. Perhaps this piece, he would set aside and keep with him for a time. He

closed his eyes, trying to fool himself into believing she was still with him, but he just couldn't make it so. Emotion drew up in his throat, and before he realized, he was sobbing into her white linen nightgown. Uncontrollable sobs forced him to the floor, where he began to pray for deliverance of the pain and emptiness that now consumed him.

From across the hall, in Mira's room, Hannah could hear Eli sobbing, and wondered if he was trying to say goodbye to Lydia. She knew that letting go of his emotions would help him heal, but it brought tears to her eyes to listen to him. She felt bad, and wanted to go to him, but she didn't want to interfere or overwhelm him. She knew that marrying her was the last thing he wanted to do, but she respected him for honoring Lydia's dying wish for Mira.

Dropping to her knees beside the cradle, she placed a hand on the sleeping baby and began to pray.

Danki, dear Lord for finally blessing me with a boppli. Help me to be a good fraa to Eli, and give him the strength to overcome his loss. Bless him with a love for his boppli so she can grow up knowing her vadder. Give me the strength to be patient with him in this unsure time, and to step aside if need-be to allow him time with Mira.

Wiping fresh tears from her eyes, a deafening crash from the other room startled her from her prayer. The raucous continued, followed by low grumbling, but she couldn't quite make out his muffled words.

He was angry.

As a midwife, she was familiar with the stages of grief, and he was certainly exercising his discontent with his wife's death. Thankfully, Mira slept soundly, oblivious to the turmoil in her home.

Another crash rent the quiet night; she had her work cut out for her if he didn't clean up the messes he was now making. The noises moved to the hall, where it sounded as if he was dragging the furniture from the room. She didn't dare poke her head out into the hallway to see for herself, but she could only imagine that he was clearing the room of anything that would remotely remind him of his wife. When he'd offered the room to her, she wanted to tell him she was content to remain where she was, but she didn't want to start off her marriage by undermining whatever efforts he would make to accommodate her in his home.

More noise and another loud crash woke Mira. Hannah tried to pick her up before she let out a scream, but she wasn't successful. She rocked her and whispered to her it was alright, holding her close, hoping it would console her,

but it would seem she was ready for another bottle. She would give anything if she didn't have to go out into the hall and face Eli in his state of grief, but it seemed inevitable.

Before she reached the door, he knocked lightly and let himself in. "I heard the crying," he began with downcast eyes. "I would like to move the furniture—perhaps while you feed her."

She didn't want to question him, so she simply nodded and walked past him to go down to the kitchen. She hadn't missed his puffy, red eyes that he'd tried to hide. Her heart ached for him, but she was powerless to help him. She would be supportive, but he would have to walk this journey alone for the most part. Though she wished she could relieve him from all of his hurt, he would have to feel it and work his way through it, while she supported him in the background—perhaps without his knowledge. She would never overstep her boundaries with him, but she would do everything she could to make his life easier.

As she reached the landing at the bottom of the stairs, she could hear him dragging what sounded like the bed from Mira's room across the hall to his bedroom. She felt funny taking the room from him, but she supposed he had no desire to sleep in there anymore. She only wished he wasn't determined to live in the *dawdi haus* even after their *wedding*.

She knew it wasn't a real marriage, or that he would want to share a room with her, but she would feel safer if he was in the main house. It had been too quiet the last few nights, except for the soft breaths from Mira in the cradle next to her. If not for that, she'd have been full of anxiety, she was certain. She wasn't used to being alone in a house, but she was prepared to get used to it. She wouldn't back out of the agreement now with Eli—not just because she didn't want to live alone. She'd chosen to be Mira's mother, and it was a sacrifice she would make for her.

Hannah hummed to Mira while she heated the goat's milk on the stove for her bottle. Upstairs, Eli continued to make noise, and she was determined not to go back up there until he came down. She felt terrible about what he was doing; she knew he was only trying to accommodate her, and it made her feel like she was putting him out. The last thing she wanted was for him to feel uncomfortable in his own home, but he'd made the decision to move into the *dawdi haus.* He'd also made the decision to marry her, and there would be no turning back now. The two of them would be the only ones who had to know it was a marriage of convenience only, and she would do her best not to let the situation be known to anyone else for fear it could compromise his standing in the

community. She would honor him as if she was a real wife, even if it could never be.

Chapter 8

Eli wrung his hands as he cringed through the two-hour ceremony that now tied him to Hannah for the rest of his life. He thought about that for a moment, and wondered if he could endure being a widower again. He hadn't thought it would happen to him and Lydia, but here he was, marrying another woman just three days after her death. He regretted making the promise to her, wondering if he hadn't, if she would still be alive. Had she given up because she was content that he and the child would be taken care of in her absence? Had it been his promise that had caused her to let go of this life?

Hannah glanced over at Eli, ignoring the words being spoken by the Bishop, and

wondering how other couples managed to stand through the lengthy ceremony. Were they all so in love that the time flew by? For her, it dragged on relentlessly as she worried with each sour expression from Eli that he was about to speak up and put an end to their wedding vows.

If he changed his mind before the Bishop finished, it would humiliate her beyond all reason, and she would lose her only chance at being a mother. She would never be able to live in the community and watch Mira grow up without being able to be her *mamm.*

She lifted her eyes and ran a prayer through her mind, continuing to drown out the Bishop's words that didn't really apply to her since she wasn't really going to be married after all was said and done—at least not in the biblical sense.

Danki Lydia for trusting me to be a mamm to your boppli, she prayed silently. *Please give your husband the strength to go through with this marriage to me. I'll do my best to take care of him and your wee one the same way you would, and I promise I'll make you proud...if you just keep me from being humiliated right now. Whisper in his ear that it's alright to marry me...whisper to him from Heaven...*

Her thoughts drifted back to the Bishop as he finished the ceremony, uniting the two of them

until death parted them. She let out a sigh of relief that he was bound to her now, and that she would indeed be Mira's *mamm.* Tears welled up in her throat as the reality of it hit her.

She was a *mamm.*

Never mind that she was also a *fraa,* because she knew it could never be more than a marriage of necessity.

Eli excused himself immediately after the Bishop announced them, leaving Hannah to deal with the sympathetic stares that would surely be followed by a lot of gossip. She ignored the watchful eyes of the single women in the community, feeling awkward at best, but her main concern was Mira, who could be heard crying, and she thought for a moment Eli might go to her, but he walked past her and his family as he disappeared into the *dawdi haus.* He'd insisted that the wedding take place at his home, and now she understood why. She supposed he deserved his solace; after all, he'd had to force himself to marry her, and she knew that. It didn't make her feel any better about the situation, but surely the community had some understanding for him and his time of grief. She was simply going to be grateful he went through with the ceremony, and not worry about him. She would give him all the space he needed, and she would concentrate on

taking care of Mira. After all, that's the only reason he married her.

Hannah went to the baby, and her new mother-in-law handed the baby over to her and kissed her on the cheek. "*Wilkum* to the *familye,*" she said to Hannah. "I know the circumstances aren't the best, but in time, Eli will open his heart to you."

She hadn't thought of that. Would he *eventually* expect her to be a proper wife in every way to him? She'd been willing to accept that when she planned to marry Jonas, but she'd had time to court him and was close enough friends with him to consider it. With Eli, they hadn't had many dates before Lydia came along and stole his affections away from her. The thought of it pricked her heart; had she loved him more than she'd allowed herself to admit?

Holding fast to Mira, she made her way into the kitchen to warm up some milk for a bottle, her mother-in-law on her heels. Thinking back on the times she'd spent with the woman after Ellie had left for her *rumspringa*, was it possible she'd felt cheated that Eli had recently married Lydia? A strange feeling welled up in her, and she pushed it down.

Frau Yoder put a hand on Hannah's shoulder, startling her from her reverie. "You

seem suddenly troubled. Did I say the wrong thing out there in the yard?"

Hannah waited for some of the ladies to gather their dishes of food from the oven and go outside to the tables that were set up for the wedding meal.

"*Nee,*" she said quietly. "I believe I was just thinking about everything and I got a little overwhelmed."

She could not confide in Eli's mother that she'd just realized she loved him, and had been suppressing it for almost two years. Or perhaps she'd felt the rush of love when he'd whooshed by her after their vows had been spoken? Whichever it was, it didn't matter. She loved Eli—her new husband, and she would wait patiently for him to return that love.

Chapter 9

Eli walked into the kitchen in the midst of all the women guests for the wedding dinner feeling as awkward as he could be. He heard whispers, but ignored them despite the strong urge to make them leave his home. The last thing he wanted was to be the subject of gossip among the women in the community. He knew they expected him to stay close to Hannah's side, but he wanted to go back to the *dawdi haus* and hide until the day was over and everyone went home. But that was not what was expected of him, and he knew he had to at least go through the motions. Surely he could get through one day. After that, he could go back to the solitude of the *dawdi haus* where his heart was safe from breaking. He

glanced at Hannah, who managed a weak smile, but he couldn't return it.

His *mamm* pulled him into a hug and drew him into the other room, while Hannah stayed behind, trying desperately not to cry in front of her guests. Thankfully, her younger sister, Rachel, stayed close to her the entire day—mostly because she was so enamored with Mira.

"Now that you're a *mamm,* are you going to let me come over and help you with the *boppli?"*

"Jah," Hannah replied. "You know you're always *wilkum* here."

She handed the sleeping baby over to her sister so she could remove the rolls from the oven. She felt awkward, even though this was her house and her kitchen now, but she could feel the eyes on her backside of women she used to count as friends. Some of them were jealous because Eli had been for two days the most eligible catch in the community in a while. Some were simply nosy, busy-bodies who loved nothing more than to have something to talk about to spice up their own dull lives.

"Can you please excuse me?" Rachel said to them. "I need a private moment with *mei schweschder."*

Hannah felt a spark of relief as she kept her back to the women while they filed out through the kitchen door and out into the yard. She watched them from the kitchen window, their expressions unhappy, as they seemed to be voicing their dislike for being ushered out of the house by a teen.

She turned around and suppressed a giggle.

"*Danki* for rescuing me from that awkwardness," she whispered to Rachel. "I couldn't take their stares or their whispering for another minute!"

"Your marriage is none of their business. It's between you and Eli. I heard some of the stuff they were saying. Is it true you're only married to him to take care of the *boppli?"*

Hannah searched for the best words to explain to her little sister. "For now," she said. "Until his heart heals."

"I heard them saying he won't go anywhere near his own *boppli."*

"He's grieving right now, Rachel. Sometimes, when adults are grieving, they need time to get over that hurt before they can spend too much time with others. He loves Mira, or he wouldn't have married me so she could have a *mamm.* It was a great sacrifice for him to marry

me when he's still grieving the way he is, but he did what was best for her."

"So you're not really his *fraa?"*

"Nee," Hannah said sadly. "At least not the way I would be if he was in love with me."

"But you love him, don't you?" she asked.

She cast her eyes down, hiding the blush at her naïve sister's comment.

"Does he know that you love him?"

"*Nee*," Hannah said quietly. "He isn't ready to know that yet."

Ellie walked into the kitchen just then with little Katie who was fussing. "I hope I'm not banned from the house like Naomi and her friends," she said with a chuckle.

"Is that what they said?" Rachel asked. "*Busy-bodies*!"

"Rachel would you mind taking Katie up to Mira's room with you and putting her down for a nap?"

She rolled her eyes. "I can take a hint."

"*Danki*," Hannah called after her as she left the room.

Ellie pulled Hannah into a hug. "We are sisters now."

Hannah began to weep quietly onto her friend's shoulder. "*Ach,* it wasn't supposed to happen this way."

"I know, and I'm sorry, but I know how much you love my brother. I never really got to know Lydia since I was gone right after their wedding, but you, I do know, and I know what a big heart you have. If anyone can help Eli get his heart back and be a father to Mira, I know you can."

"*Danki,* that means a lot to me."

Ellie pulled away and smiled. "Don't cry anymore; it's your wedding day."

She sniffled. "It wasn't a *real* wedding."

Ellie scrunched her brow. "Of course it was. You'll see, my brother will come to love you just as soon as he's had time to process everything. He'll appreciate you being here for him and for his *dochder*—for your *dochder* now. You and I are sisters now and we are both *mamms,* and Katie has a new cousin. Be happy. It will all work out; God has a plan for you and your new family."

Hannah wiped her tears and forced a smile, just as Eli and his *mamm* entered the room.

He held a shaky hand out to her. "Let's go out and eat with our guests."

Hannah placed her hand in his, the warmth of his skin making her flesh tingle well past her elbow. She followed him out into the yard, where it was evident by their expressions that she was the envy of all the single women in the community.

Chapter 10

Eli stepped into the kitchen with a fresh pail of goat's milk for the *boppli.* He intended to milk the goat for Hannah to keep her out of the barn as much as possible, in order to avoid having to make small talk with her that felt forced and uncomfortable. She stood at the stove dishing up scrambled eggs and bacon onto a plate, and turned when he entered the room.

He paused, feeling awkward when she handed him the food.

She was being kind to him—being a wife—and he didn't like it. It only made him feel even more guilty that he could not be a husband to her the way she deserved. He cared for her, but

he would not allow himself to love her, for fear it would betray his wife's memory.

It was only a meal, and she'd made it for him willingly. He owed her nothing for it. After all, he was providing her with a home, and had basically given his child to her. He grumbled a *Danki* under his breath, and took the plate of food out to the *dawdi haus* to eat it. He hated seeming rude and ungrateful, but he was not up for socializing with her.

She'd not said a word to stop him from leaving the house, and he preferred it that way. Having to keep up appearances yesterday at the wedding meal had exhausted him to the point he almost couldn't get out of bed this morning, but he knew that keeping himself busy on his farm would also keep his mind too busy to dwell on his grief.

With Eli out of the house, Hannah sat at the kitchen table alone and choked down the meal around the lump in her throat. She knew he hadn't meant to hurt her feelings, and so she forgave him, but that didn't mean it didn't hurt anyway. If it was possible, she almost felt more lonely married than she had when she was single.

She rose from the table and went to the sink with her dishes. Looking out at the *dawdi haus,* she knew she'd have to go in there after he returned to the barn to resume his chores to get

his dirty dishes and clothes. She would continue to cook and clean for him, and take care of his child, hoping that someday he would return her love. If he didn't, she prayed God would remove the love in her heart for him to keep her heart from breaking. She feared her love would continue to grow for him and he would never let himself love her back.

After running water in the sink, she heard Mira crying in her cradle in the other room. Hannah had brought it downstairs so she could cook, not wanting to be out of earshot of the infant. She wondered how new mothers managed to get anything done; so far, she had a lot of things started, but nothing finished—unless she counted the morning meal, but that was nothing short of a disaster.

She went to her child and changed her diaper, then held her close and kissed her, feeling ashamed for complaining the least little bit about her husband. Though he might not ever be ready to be a husband in the traditional sense, he'd given her the best gift a man could give a woman; he'd given her a child to care for and love, and that was a far better life than she would have had if Eli hadn't rescued her from becoming a spinster.

As she prepared Mira's bottle, she reflected on a prayer she'd prayed not too long

ago asking God to bless her with a husband. He'd not only blessed her with a husband, but a child too. But was it all part of God's plan for Lydia to have to pass away in order for her to get what she wanted in life? Tears welled up in her eyes as she thought about it.

Dear Lord, did my prayers bring Lydia's death? Forgive me if my prayers were selfish.

Deep down, she knew better, and she was determined she wouldn't waste even a day of the blessing God bestowed on her by dwelling on how it was He blessed her.

She feared if she gave in to such foolish notions it would increase the guilt that already weighed her down.

Chapter 11

Hannah fashioned a sling from a bed-sheet, wrapping Mira in it, and tying it close to her so she wouldn't have to lug around the laundry basket while trying to balance the *boppli* in her arms. With the wee one tucked against her heart, she pulled the ends of the sheet over both arms and crossed it over her shoulders, tying it at her waist. She prayed that hearing her heart, Mira would be soothed by it and get used to hearing it. It was a mother's heartbeat that soothed a fussy infant, and she hoped Mira would be comforted by it, and come to know it as her own *mamm*.

Though it was Saturday, Hannah was determined to get ahead of the laundry that had piled up for the past week, hoping to be finished

by the end of the day on Monday. It was beginning to get a little chilly, being the second week of November, and so she placed a bonnet on Mira's head, assuming Lydia had crocheted it.

Heading out to the *dawdi haus,* her first stop would be to gather Eli's things. She worried he would think she was overstepping her boundaries, and so she prayed he wouldn't cross her path while she was in there.

He'd spent most of the day tinkering with something. All she knew was the constant sound of a hammer, and wondered what he could be building. Perhaps it was a new stall for the horse that was about to foal. With winter coming, it would need space inside the barn.

She had noticed that Lydia had not finished canning all of her vegetables, and she hoped Eli would not be upset if she finished the chore. She'd come across the unfinished task in the root cellar when she was searching for staples to prepare for the week's meals. She thought perhaps he wouldn't even notice, since he'd been avoiding her as much as possible.

With him spending so much time in the barn and living in the *dawdi haus*, it almost seemed comical to her that she felt more like a single mom than a married woman. She hoped that time would heal his wounds, and that he would begin to spend time with his daughter.

Even if he didn't want to see her or be a husband to her in any way, she prayed that he would begin to be a father to Mira.

Setting down the basket on the floor of the bedroom in the *dawdi haus*, Hannah began to strip the bed so she could change the linens. She almost missed the nightgown that was tucked under his pillow, and realized it belonged to Lydia. Her heart ached at the thought of him pining over a dead woman, but she supposed it would take some time for him to recover from his loss. She couldn't imagine the sort of hurt he was feeling from losing someone so dear to him, but it wasn't because she hadn't experienced loss in her own life. Still, losing a spouse had to be much different than the loss of a parent or extended family such as a cousin.

She retrieved the nightgown from the laundry basket, and folded it neatly, placing it back under the pillow. Then, she proceeded to pick up his laundry from the hamper in the bathroom. Once she gathered all his things, she retrieved his dirty dishes from the sink in the kitchen and place them on top of the laundry in the basket. She hoisted the basket up onto her hip, and the dishes clanked, startling Mira, but she quickly relaxed again and didn't wake Fully.

Relieved, Hannah was careful to be quieter as she exited the *dawdi haus* out into the

cold November air. She tucked the small knitted blanket over the baby's head and hands that stuck outside the sling to keep the cool air from giving her a chill. Hannah knew it wasn't too chilly for her, but babies were much more sensitive to the cold than adults were, and she aimed to guard her from the gusts of wind that threatened to bring snow from the Northern sky.

Once inside the main house, she went to the modern laundry room where she'd washed her clothes for the past couple of weeks that she'd stayed as a guest. Eli had done well for himself by installing a windmill and solar panels on the roof of the main house, the *dawdi haus*, and the barn. Those things provided enough electricity to run the home efficiently. And though she had a modern gas-powered dryer, she preferred to hang the wash outside, even in the cold crisp air of late autumn. She'd used the clothesline several times already, and had familiarized herself enough with where everything was in the home. Since she'd taken care of Lydia in her last days of her pregnancy, she was grateful she'd had that time to acclimate herself with the home. It made the transition easier now that she was the woman of the house.

Stopping in the kitchen to drop off the dishes in the sink, she took the time to run some hot water so they could soak. Eli had left them there since the previous morning, and he had not

returned for another meal that day. After missing the noon meal, however, Hannah had slipped into the *dawdi haus* and put a plate of food in the refrigerator for him to have for dinner. She was happy to see that he'd used the dishes and he'd eaten the meal that she'd left for him. She knew that keeping up his strength was important right now. If she could help it, she would not allow him to become run-down. She would feed him well and continue to pray for him that strength and peace would get him through this tough time. She didn't enjoy invading his privacy, but it was necessary in order to keep him from wasting away and wallowing in his grief.

Eli took a break from building the stall in the barn, and decided to get himself a drink of water, and he needed to use the bathroom. As he entered the *dawdi haus*, he noticed that things had been moved. Hannah had been in here again, and left him feeling a bit invaded. When he walked into the bedroom, panic filled him when he saw the bare mattress. He rushed to the bed and dropped to his knees grabbing his pillow and pulling it to him. Then he noticed that Lydia's nightgown was still there. It was folded neatly, and had been replaced back under the pillow. Hannah had respected him enough to put it back where she'd found it, and that meant everything to him right now.

He breathed a sigh of relief as he pulled the garment toward him and buried his face in it, breathing a prayer that God would relieve him from his grief and to make him the sort of man Hannah could be proud to call a husband, and Mira could be proud to call him *vadder*.

Chapter 12

Hannah hadn't expected to run into Eli when she returned to the *dawdi haus* to change the bedding. With Mira still strapped to the front of her, and fresh linens in both arms, she hadn't thought about the need to knock on the door.

Taking him by surprise, Eli scrambled to his feet, trying to hide his embarrassment by wadding up the nightgown and stuffing it into the dresser drawer. He'd been so engrossed in prayer that he hadn't heard her approach. He didn't quite know why it mattered that she knew he had ahold of the garment, especially since she already knew it was there.

She immediately tried to excuse herself and back out of the room, but he was already

awkwardly moving past her to get out of the house. As he brushed by her, he glanced down at the *boppli* laying against her, his expression quickly fell, his eyes cast down toward the floor.

Her arm tingled from the warmth of his bare forearm brushing against hers, and she was glad he'd left the room so he couldn't see her blushing now. She prayed he wasn't angry with her for barging in on him. she'd tried to apologize, but he didn't seem interested in hearing it; he seemed to preoccupied with getting away from her and Mira.

She swallowed the lump in her throat and asked God to keep her from taking it personally. She was certain the tufts of blond curls on Mira's head painfully reminded him of Lydia. She could see the pain in his eyes when he looked at the child.

Hannah set to work quickly to make the bed so she didn't have to invade his space any more than she had to. As for the nightgown; she would leave it in the drawer where he left it.

When she finished, Mira began to wake up, and she went back to the main house to get a bottle ready. Again, she ran into Eli, who had brought in a fresh pail of goat's milk for Mira.

"*Danki,*" she said softly.

He nodded, taking a long look at the infant before exiting the house.

At least he was able to really look at her this time, Hannah thought happily. *Danki, Lord, for small miracles.*

A knock at the door made her wonder if he'd forgotten something, but she didn't think he would knock on his own door, would he?

She hollered "*Kume,*" while she poured the milk into Mira's bottle.

The door opened behind her, and she turned to see who it was. Hannah fell back against the counter, dropping the bottle of milk when she caught herself from falling to the floor. Her heart sank as she gazed upon the *Englisch* woman.

"You must be Hannah," she said.

Lydia!

Hannah couldn't find her voice.

"I'm here for my sister's baby," she said, looking at Mira. "This must be her."

"*What?*" Hannah said.

Did she just say she was here for the boppli—as in to take her away? Did she say she was Lydia's schweschder?

Hannah was having a hard time looking past the identical resemblance to Lydia.

"My Mennonite cousins called me only yesterday, or I'd have been here sooner," she said, reaching for Mira.

Before she realized, the woman had managed to lift Mira from the bunting she'd had tied to her.

Hannah looked at her and quickly surveyed the door, wondering if the woman intended to really *take* Mira. Surely Eli would stop her, wouldn't he?

The woman looked at her and frowned. "I'm guessing you didn't know Lydia had a twin? I'm Alana. I've been shunned because I left after taking the baptism. The community wouldn't even let me attend my parent's funerals with the rest of the family. I wasn't allowed to attend my own sister's wedding, and now I've missed *her* funeral too, but they won't keep me from her baby!"

"I can't speak for *mei mann,* Eli," Hannah said, feeling suddenly vulnerable and threatened.

"Yes, I was told my sister's husband remarried two days ago!" she said, her lip curling up at the sight of Hannah. "What kind of man remarries so soon after his wife dies?"

"Your *schweschder* made him promise to marry me shortly after giving birth…so that Mira would have a *mamm,"* Hannah said defensively.

"*Mira?"* Alana asked. "Whose decision was it to name that child after my mother?"

"Lydia named the child. I was the midwife in attendance."

"So it's *your* fault my sister is dead!"

Tears welled up in Hannah's eyes. "*Nee,* Mira was breech, and Lydia was bleeding too much. By the time the ambulance arrived, she was already gone."

"Who called for the ambulance?" Alana asked.

"Eli and I *both* insisted, even though Lydia was against it."

"I was also told that Eli won't even have anything to do with my sister's baby," Alana continued.

Was she *looking* to find fault in order to give her a reason to take the child away?

"He's grieving," Hannah said, defending him.

"The child clearly needs a mother!"

Hannah pulled the fresh bottle of milk from the pan of hot water on the stove and tested the warmth against her wrist. Mira had begun to cry, and she held her arms out to take the child.

Alana snatched the bottle from her. “I’m perfectly capable of feeding my sister’s baby!”

Hannah didn’t say a word, but stayed close in case she didn’t calm down in the stranger’s arms.

She sat in a chair at the kitchen table and placed the bottle in Mira’s mouth. She began to gulp it down.

“When’s the last time you fed her?” Alana asked. “She’s acting like she’s starving!”

“She had a bottle a little over two hours ago,” Hannah answered calmly.

Alana leaned down and kissed Mira’s head, closing her eyes and smelling her head. “I should be the logical one to raise my sister’s child—not a *stranger.”*

Mira looked content in Alana’s arms, and it brought tears to Hannah’s eyes. Was she going to attempt to take her away?

“I’m guessing since my sister’s husband is living in the *dawdi haus,* the two of you haven’t *consummated* your marriage.”

Hannah hung her head out of embarrassment at the woman’s forward statement.

“I didn’t think so,” Alana said. “In that case, I can go to the Bishop and have your marriage annulled.”

Panic rose up in Hannah. Could she do that?

"I'll marry Eli and raise my sister's baby. After a lengthy confession, I'll be welcomed back into the community, and when I marry him, I won't be shunned anymore."

Just then, Eli walked into the door. He'd not wanted to enter the house and run into Hannah again, but he needed to find out who owned the car that was blocking him from leaving his driveway to go into town.

There in front of him was his child in the arms of…

His heart drummed against his ribs, and his breath caught in his throat. His legs felt suddenly wobbly as he stumbled forward, knocking over the chair in his path.

Lydia?

Chapter 13

Alana looked at the man in front of her, wondering about his clean-shaven face. Was this her sister's husband? If so, why had he dishonored his wife by shaving his beard? Was it because Hannah hadn't become his wife in the biblical sense?

Eli looked to Hannah, who looked just as befuddled as he was by the mysterious woman's presence. It was obvious to him that she was the twin sister his wife had mentioned a time or two during their short-lived courtship and marriage.

"Are you Alana?" he asked.

"Yes I am," she answered. "I'm guessing by your reaction to me that you must be Eli."

"Jah," he replied.

"We have a lot to talk about," she said. "Will you take me out to visit my sister's grave?"

He looked to Hannah. "Can you be ready to go so I can take her to the graveside?"

"I'd like to go with just you," Alana said.

"It wouldn't be proper to go without an escort," Eli said.

"Then we'll take Mira with us."

Hannah's heart sank. Was this woman about to take her whole world away from her?

"Nee," he replied. "She's *mei fraa."*

"That's exactly what I want to talk to you about," she said as she set Mira's bottle down and lifted her onto her shoulder to burp her.

Again, Eli looked to Hannah. "Are you ready to go?"

She would not argue with the man, but it was obvious Alana didn't want her to go. She nodded to him, deciding to obey her husband.

Grabbing Mira's knitted bonnet and sweater, she tried to coax the infant out from Alana's arms, but she merely held her hand out to take the knitted things. Hannah picked up the thick quilt and handed it to the woman while she put on her black cloak and bonnet.

"Maybe I should warm an extra bottle," she said, hoping to stall a little for time.

She didn't know why, but perhaps she hoped Eli would make her go alone once she left the room to make the bottle. Alana followed her, so that plan backfired on her.

"You'll need to move your car," he said to Alana.

"Why don't we just take my car?"

Hannah looked to Eli to give a quick excuse, and he didn't disappoint her.

"We don't have a car-seat for the *boppli,*" he said calmly.

She smiled. "I've got one! It'll be much faster if we take my car."

Hannah nodded slightly to him. She was all for getting this trip over with quickly and getting rid of Alana so she could be rid of her.

"I'll get my things out of the car while you put the horse and buggy away."

"Your *things?*" Hannah asked.

Alana looked around her. "Surely this house has an extra room that I could stay in."

Hannah kept quiet hoping Eli would tell her to leave, but this time he disappointed her.

"You're more than *wilkum* to stay here during your visit."

Then he disappeared to put away his horse.

She knew it was their way not to turn a relative away, but she was a shunned woman. Surely he wasn't going to let her stay on for an extended period of time—except that he wasn't there during that part of the conversation and didn't know what she'd said to her.

Surely he *had* to know, didn't he?

She would not be able to say anything now, and so she kept her mouth shut and went along with Alana pushing her around. It made her angry, but she would let it go until Eli fixed it.

With Eli and Alana both outside, she prayed that the woman would not come between her and her husband and child.

But then she had a thought.

Was it selfish of her to keep Mira away from her blood relative? Was it really better for Lydia's sister to raise her? Surely Lydia would have mentioned her with her dying breath and make Eli promise to marry Alana instead of her if she trusted her, wouldn't she? Perhaps she didn't trust her estranged sister, and for that reason, Hannah would keep a close eye on her.

Let your will be done, Lord, she prayed.

Chapter 14

Alana brought her suitcases into the house and dropped them on the floor beside the kitchen door. Then, she extended her arms out to Mira. "I'll put her in the car-seat."

Hannah let her take the baby from her. She reasoned that she was, after all, Mira's *aenti.* So she let it go—for now. Since Alana seemed a bit bossy, she had to wonder why it was that Lydia had not warned Eli about her. Had she forgotten about her when she was taking her last breath, or had she not thought her own sister would pose a threat to her daughter's future? Either way, Hannah had made a promise to Lydia that she would be a *mamm* to her *boppli,* and she was

determined to protect her at all cost—even from her own *aenti.*

Eli took his time putting *Moose* in the barn, hoping by stalling, he could come up with a way to get Alana out of his mind. When he'd set his eyes on her, she'd taken his breath away. She looked so much like Lydia, it was tough for him to suppress the urge to pull her into his arms and make himself forget his wife was gone. But could he really fool himself like that for more than a few minutes?

Realizing what he was thinking, he dropped to his knees beside a large bale of hay. *Lord, forgive me for thinking about holding Alana when I'm married to Hannah. Help me to pull myself together and face Lydia's death before I destroy my future and the future of Hannah and Mira. Help me to figure a way out of the mess I'm in, and show me your plan for my life. Let your will be done, Lord.*

Once Mira was all strapped in, Eli came out of the barn, his expression heavy. Hannah climbed in next to the baby in the back seat, and Eli surprised her by getting in beside her.

"Wouldn't you feel more comfortable up front with me, Eli?" Alana asked. "It would give us a chance to talk."

"Nee," he said politely. "I can hear you just fine from back here, and I prefer to sit with *mei familye."*

He felt Hannah relax beside him, and her closeness sent a strange shiver through him. the warmth of her thigh that touched his made it tough for him to concentrate on anything else.

What was happening to him?

His emotions were all over the place.

He reasoned that it was because they were about to go to the graveside of his beloved Lydia, and he was simply still in shock from her death.

But it was more than that, and he knew it.

He was certain Hannah could sense it too.

Resting his elbow against the window, he leaned his chin on his palm and stared out the window as they passed farm after farm.

His neighbors.

The trees were nearly bare, and the miles of farmland was littered with colorful leaves. Winter would be upon them within days, and the snow would close them in for the season. Would he be able to bear the cold of the *dawdi haus?* It wasn't that the house lacked a fireplace, because it had a nice stone hearth. It was the lack of love and family that the place represented. He didn't like being all alone out there, and it would get

even lonelier with a long winter separating him from his only child.

He let his gaze wander to Mira. She was truly a beautiful baby. Her curly blond hair reminded him of Lydia, and her blue eyes mirrored his own. He reached across Hannah and touched Mira's small hand. Her milky skin was warm enough to melt his heart.

He removed his hand, glancing at Hannah. Tears filled her eyes, and she smiled warmly at him. He forced a smile, but it wasn't as tough as he thought it was going to be.

Alana pulled into the cemetery with a loud sigh. "Which way?"

Eli pointed and told her the section marking to look for. She pulled into the lot beside the row of graves where Lydia was laid to rest. Turning around in her seat, she asked Eli to take her to the grave.

He placed a hand on Hannah's arm.

There was that strange shiver again.

"*Kume,*" he said to his wife.

She unbuckled Mira and lifted her into her arms, and slid across the seat to exit the car. She walked beside her husband as they made their way to the gravesite. It was an emotional setting that made Hannah feel uncomfortable.

Alana fell to the ground and began to weep, repeatedly apologizing to Lydia for not being there for her, while Eli worked his jaw to keep it clenched against the tears that would surely fall if he didn't keep his emotions in check.

Strong frigid winds brought dark clouds swiftly overhead, and Hannah worried icy rain would soon be upon them.

"Perhaps I should take the *boppli* back to the car out of the wind," Hannah said, interrupting Alana's confession to her sister.

Alana jumped up from the grave and wiped her eyes and looked at Eli. "I should go with her to help protect my sister's baby. I'll give you some time here, Eli."

He nodded and the two women headed toward the car. When they were nearly there, Alana stopped and handed Hannah the keys.

"You know, I forgot to leave a memento at my sister's grave. You get the baby in the car, and I'll be right back."

Hannah accepted the keys, though she was certain it was an excuse for Alana to converse with her husband about going to the Bishop regarding their marriage. After strapping Mira in the car-seat, she turned around and watched as the woman seemed to be deep in the middle of a long lecture with Eli.

After a few minutes, however, Eli nodded to her and began to walk away, and it appeared to anger Alana, who followed closely on his heels, apparently chattering about her plans to get her way.

Hannah felt a sharp pain at her ribcage, heartburn souring her stomach over the woman's actions. It seemed she was determined to have her cause heard, and she didn't seem like the type to back down. Worry turned to fear in Hannah's stomach, but Eli's expression remained calm as he slid into the back seat of Alana's car next to her. She looked to her husband for comfort, and he gave it to her with a simple gesture.

He placed his hand on top of hers, tapping lightly only twice before removing it, but it was enough to let her know he was not going to stand for Lydia's sister getting in the way of her last wishes for her family.

Chapter 15

They rode back to the house in silence, and Hannah's heart beat faster the closer they came to the farm she wasn't sure she'd be calling *home* very much longer if Alana had any say in it.

Eli unexpectedly took Mira from Hannah and walked into the house with the two of them, and then handed her back once they got inside the kitchen. Reaching down, he picked up Alana's bags and began to walk outside with them.

"Where are you taking my things?" she asked impatiently. "I plan on staying here."

He turned and looked her in the eye. "You can stay in the *dawdi haus.*"

She twisted up her face and planted her hands on her hips in a huff. "I'm not living out there with you. We aren't married yet!"

"We aren't going to be married because I'm already married—to Hannah. And I won't be living out there either; I'm moving *mei* things back in the main *haus* with *mei familye.*"

Hannah's heart thumped harder at the thought of Eli being in the house with her. Surely he intended to sleep in one of the four bedrooms upstairs—unless he decided he wanted to move her out of his own room so he could return to it. Either way, she would accommodate him; after all, it was *his* house.

"That isn't going to stop me from going to see the Bishop in the morning!" she called after him.

Eli kept walking with her bags, set them inside the door and haphazardly tossed his few things on top of the bed, wrapped it up in his quilt, and grabbed his pillow with his other hand.

"I'll send Hannah out with some clean linens and towels for you," he said as he took his things from the bathroom. Luckily, he hadn't moved his things fully into the small cottage, or it would have been much too time-consuming to gather his things, and he intended not to make another trip out to the *dawdi haus*. He wouldn't

step foot back in the place until Alana was long-gone, and he hoped that would be soon.

It wasn't that he intended to keep her from seeing her niece, but if she meant trouble for his wife or child, he would have no other choice but to make her leave. A sudden rush of responsibility washed over him, leaving him feeling strange about his change of heart where Hannah and Mira were concerned. He knew deep down it was his duty to protect them. He felt compelled to in such a strong way—a way that almost made him think he loved them both.

He entered the main house, his arms full. Walking past Hannah, he went up the stairs and hesitated before going into the room he shared with Lydia. It seemed like an entire lifetime ago that he was in that room with her holding her hand as she slipped away from him, but now, as he entered the room; he didn't recognize any of it.

Everything was different.

In the corner, Mira's cradle rested on a braided rug he didn't recognize. Doilies and late-blooming wild flowers propped in Mason jars rested on both lamp tables, fancy oil lamps in place of the copper ones that were there before. In general, the room looked *feminine,* but he set his things on top of the yellow and white wedding-ring quilt he figured Hannah must have sewn for her dowry. All in all, the room was fresh and

sunny in appearance, the yellows adding a cheerfulness to the room. It looked so different; he thought he might just be able to be comfortable in the room again.

Hannah entered the room just then with Mira asleep on her shoulder.

He looked at her holding his child and suddenly remembered what made him begin courting her at a time that seemed like a whole other lifetime ago. It was her big heart that appealed to him.

She set the baby in the cradle without a word to him, and then eyed his things on the bed. Immediately, she went to the dresser and began to remove her things from the drawer. "I'll have *mei* things packed quickly, but I'll need to have you move the cradle across the hall for me."

He walked over to her and placed a hand on hers, stopping her from packing. "I want you to stay."

Her breath hitched, and she bit her bottom lip. Surely he didn't mean what he said.

Chapter 16

Hannah wrung her hands nervously when Eli asked her to sit beside him on the bed. She knew he was her husband, and she didn't fear him, but she'd not been in this situation, and he'd been married before already.

"I know I said I would not be a husband to you in any way, but it seems Alana is challenging that. I hate to even ask to place such a burden on you, but I'm afraid until she leaves, we are going to have to make it *appear* that we are married in every sense of the way—if you understand my meaning."

He was being kind and she understood, but it made her nervous to put on pretenses. She nodded nonetheless.

"I'll need to stay in the room with you and Mira at night—but I'll sleep on the floor."

"That won't be necessary," she said. "I trust you."

He cleared his throat nervously. It was evident he wasn't through talking about the problem.

"She didn't just threaten to go to the Bishop; she mentioned talking to a lawyer. If you and I are not married in the traditional sense, she could pursue action to annul our marriage. At least that's what she claims. I don't think we need to consult a lawyer because she can't force me to marry her if I don't want to. I want you to know I'm dedicated to this marriage—even though it's only for convenience. I've watched you with Mira, and I believe Lydia made a wise choice when she asked you to be her *mamm.*"

His voice broke a little, and she knew it wasn't easy for him to talk about any of this.

"Danki," Hannah said softly.

"I need to know if it's alright with you if I act *affectionately* toward you around Alana so she gets the idea we are a *real couple*."

"Jah, but do you really think that'll be necessary?"

He stood up and began to put his things away in the empty dresser that he was used to using before.

"I'm afraid Alana has become even more *Englisch* than Lydia described to me, and she isn't going to take our word for it. She's going to want to see for herself that she can't break up our *familye."*

"Ach, I have a tough time understanding how she thinks she can come here and take over."

"Lydia was the last of her *familye,* and they were very close when they were *kinner* in the same *haus,* but Alana wanted to separate herself from her twin and be her own person. Lydia told me she always felt like she was her shadow, and she wanted the world to see *her* and not the two of them as one. It's not easy for me to understand either because Ellie and I are not identical twins. The only thing I do understand is the bond between twins, and I imagine it must be greater if the person is a clone of you. She believes because she is an identical replica of Lydia that she's the logical *replacement* for her, and that Mira will automatically bond with her because of it. I don't agree with that because they don't share the same heart."

He hung his head.

Hannah knew this was all too much too soon for him; it was for her too. Still, she would

trust that he knew what was best—especially if it helped her to remain Mira's *mamm.*

Chapter 17

Hannah was happy to see Rachel when she showed up to help with the evening meal. Having finished her chores at home, she'd taken the extra time to lend a hand where it was greatly needed. Not to mention the fact she knew she would feel less intimidated by Alana with her sister around. Rachel was, after all, far more outgoing than Hannah was herself, and if Alana spoke out of turn, Rachel would be the one to put her in her place. She'd always been a little mouthy that way, but she supposed it was more because of the cousins she was always hanging around. That, and her young age.

Lately, she and her cousins had talked non-stop about taking their *rumspringa*, and Hannah

dreaded the thought of it for her younger sister, whom she worried would not return if she got a taste of *Englisch* freedom, as she referred to her upcoming right-of-passage. With her birthday just around the corner, Hannah hoped that spending extra time with her and Mira would make her crave a future as an Amish wife rather than the wild and rule-free life of the *Englisch.*

"Whose car is that outside?" she asked as she bound in the door and went straight to the infant seat to pick up the baby.

"It belongs to Alana—Lydia's twin sister. She's here to cause trouble for me, so I'm glad you're here. I don't trust her."

Hannah handed her sister the baby's bottle so she could feed Mira while she finished putting her pie in the oven.

"What sort of trouble?" Rachel asked.

She wiped her hands on her apron and sat across from Rachel at the kitchen table.

"She caused Eli to move his things back in the *haus,* and he has to stay with me until she leaves."

Rachel giggled. "You're blushing!"

"We have to sleep in the same room!" Hannah said in a high pitch.

"Isn't that what married couples are supposed to do?" Rachel asked, rolling her eyes.

Hannah sighed and jumped up from her chair, crossing to the window and looking out at Alana, who was coming toward the house.

"Under normal circumstances, that would be correct," she said hastily. "But you know he isn't ready to be a husband to me, and he might never be, but she threatened to go to the Bishop and have our marriage annulled. So now we have to make it look like we are a regular married couple so she'll leave us alone! She thinks she is better-suited to be Mira's *mamm* than me. Promise me you won't say anything to her!"

"Why would I tell her?" she said. "No one is better-suited to be her *mamm* than you. Besides, it's none of her business, but I hope you know what you're getting yourself into."

"Ach, me too!"

Alana let herself into the house and reached to take the baby from Rachel, but she stopped her with a look. "I'm not finished feeding her!"

Alana whipped her head around to Hannah. "Who is she holding onto my sister's baby? Is this your nanny?"

"Nee, I'm her *schweschder,* Mira's *aenti*— the same as you!" Rachel said boldly.

"No!" Alana said through gritted teeth. "You're not the same at all. I'm blood-related and should be raising her instead of your sister, who is involved in a marriage of lies."

"It isn't lies," Rachel snapped before Hannah could say a word. "Eli needed some time to heal from his loss."

"It's only been a few days!" Alana shot back. "That's all my sister meant to him? She doesn't even get a proper mourning period from her husband?"

"It seems to me that *you* intend to take that mourning period from him—that *you* should marry him instead. Should he be a proper husband to *you* if he marries you? Or should he *grow* to love his new *fraa?*"

"Seems to me he wasted no time—or maybe he's only trying to make me *think* he has so I'll be on my way. I'm not going anywhere!"

Hannah's heart did a somersault behind her ribcage. Would nothing make this woman leave them alone?

Just then, Eli came in with some wild, yellow daisies from the meadow and handed them to Hannah, kissing her lightly on the cheek. "I thought these might look nice on the table for dinner; I know how much you like wildflowers."

"Wouldn't those be better for my sister's grave?" Alana asked, her eyes narrowed on Eli. "I noticed there aren't any flowers at her grave-side, and that's shameful, given the so-called support she has from this community."

"I believe flowers are for the living," Eli said sternly. "Your *schweschder* was not shallow like that or selfish. She would be happy knowing I've brought flowers into the house to share with *mei familye.* She also liked having fresh-picked flowers in the *haus,* and I'm going to continue to bring them—to Hannah and Mira now."

Alana marched toward the door. "I *love* how every one of you has forgotten my sister so quickly."

"It seems to me that *you* forgot her while she was still alive, and now you want to come in here and convince us you loved her so much that you want to take over everything in her life now that she's gone? Where were you when she was here with us, missing you? You could have come back home and been a guest at our wedding, and a part of her life, and even been there when she took her last breath, but you weren't. Don't come into this *haus* and try to make anyone here believe you were a *gut schweschder.* The time for that was when she was still alive."

Eli hadn't meant to be so harsh, but she'd pushed her limits with him.

Alana rushed from the house and slammed the door behind her. Hannah, who was still standing at the sink, watched her run into the *dawdi haus* with her hand over her mouth.

She was crying, and Hannah felt compelled to go to her and comfort her.

Chapter 18

"She what?" Hannah asked loudly.

"She offered me a job at her advertisement agency answering the phone and filing papers," Rachel said excitedly. "She's going to teach me how to use the computer."

"Why would you want to be around Alana?" Hannah asked. "She's selfish and worldly."

She looked at her little sister with her day-dreamy eyes, and realized that was *exactly* Alana's appeal to her. She could offer her a life she'd been craving for far too long; she and her band of wild cousins that hang out in town constantly. If her *mamm* were still alive, she knew

Rachel wouldn't be so out of control. She'd tried her best to fill her *mamm's* shoes and take care of her sister, but she had a wild streak in her that just couldn't be tamed, no matter how much punishment their *daed* threatened her with.

The only good news in Rachel's statement was that it made it sound as if Alana was thinking of leaving.

She regretted letting Rachel go to comfort her instead of going herself, but she hadn't shown up for the evening meal, and with Mira being fussy, Hannah agreed to let her sister take a plate of food to her. She hadn't paid too much attention to the time, thinking the girl had come back in the house and was washing the dishes. But once she'd put Mira down to sleep, she came back downstairs to a messy kitchen, completely devoid of her sister.

Now, she ran some dishwater in the sink and watched the girl with a farther-off look in her eyes than usual, and asked her to help with a task that held no meaning to her. She didn't want to be Amish any more than Hannah wanted to be an *Englischer.*

"*Daed* will not let you go!"

Rachel shook her head. "He told me as long as I go with the cousins, I can go, and he agreed to help me with a little money to get an

apartment. But now since I have a job waiting for me, he's sure to let me go."

Hannah sighed, knowing her *daed* didn't know what to do with Rachel any more than she did. Perhaps she'd been too caught up in her own whirlwind life to notice Rachel had grown away from her. She really thought that having her help with her new home and baby would help settle her down a bit, but it would seem it had only had the opposite effect on her. she knew there would be no stopping her if she had permission from their *daed,* and so supporting her decision would be the only thing that would keep communication open between them.

"Promise me you won't just run off without telling me goodbye," Hannah said.

Her expression fell. "I'm not even sure I'm going."

Hannah's ears perked up, though she feigned sympathy for her younger sister. "What do you mean?"

"She said several times *if* she returns. But she did say that if she doesn't, she has a friend who can take her business over and I can work for her!"

"Seems a little like an unstable promise to me," Hannah said as she sank her hands into the warm, sudsy dishwater, flinging some bubbles at

Rachel with a giggle. "Alana is just a little too wishy-washy, so promise me you won't come back here being like that."

Handing a dry towel to her sister, she turned and noticed Alana behind her. She hadn't heard the kitchen door, and wondered just how long Alana had been standing there holding her dirty dishes in her hands.

Chapter 19

Hannah rolled over to a gurgling baby beside her, and wondered how she'd gotten there. She panicked thinking she could have gotten up and put the infant in bed with her without so much as waking up. Was she really that exhausted?

When the bedroom door opened, she turned and saw Eli enter the room with a bottle for the baby. He must have put Mira in bed with her, but had she been sleeping so soundly that she hadn't heard her cry? Then she remembered finding Eli asleep in the oversized chair beside the bed, with his feet propped up on the ottoman. She'd draped a quilt over him before getting into bed. Though she was grateful he was sleeping in

the chair, she felt guilty for taking the bed when he surely had to be uncomfortable sleeping there.

She sat up and held her hand out for the bottle, but he set it down on the bedside table between the bed and the chair, then lifted his daughter from beside Hannah and sat down in the chair with her. He tucked a burp-cloth under her chin and held the bottle for her, smiling at her.

"I'm your *daed,"* he said softly. "I'm going to help take care of you, and I'm going to protect you and teach you what you need to know to grow up and be just as special as *both* your *mamms."*

Hannah could hear the shakiness of his voice, and it brought tears to her eyes that he would include her as Mira's mother. She watched him in the pale moonlight that filtered in through the sheer curtains on the windows. He was truly a handsome and loving man, and she was lucky to have him.

If it was possible, she fell even more in love with him right then and there as she continued to watch him care for his infant daughter. It was an answer to many prayers, but she still had one unanswered—that Eli would someday be able to return that love to her.

He held Mira up on his shoulder to burp her.

"How am I doing?" he asked. "I've watched you, and it seems this is what you do."

She giggled lightly. "You're doing everything right. You're going to be a *gut daed* to her."

"*Danki,*" he said. "I don't know what I was so afraid of. Loving her, I suppose. I think I was so afraid of losing her that I didn't want to get too close to her."

"That's understandable," Hannah said, propping herself up on her elbow to face him. "After *mei mamm* died, I would go to visit your *mamm* and cook with her because I needed a *mamm* so badly that I convinced myself she was the perfect replacement. But after a while, I stopped going because I was afraid she would leave me too. I suppose that helps me to be a little sympathetic for Alana."

"I suppose we should keep her in our prayers," he said as he rocked Mira.

Hannah flopped back down on her pillow and yawned, which caused Eli to yawn.

"How long before she's going to wake back up again wanting another bottle?" he asked.

She giggled. "In a couple of hours!"

"Then I better get her back in the cradle and get to sleep myself," he said. "This farm

wakes up at the same time every morning no matter how much sleep I get."

She giggled softly in agreement as she watched him place the sleeping baby gently back in her cradle.

He went to the chair and picked up the quilt, and then pivoted toward the bed where Hannah was.

Without a word, she pulled open the covers on that side of the bed inviting him in.

He slipped in the bed facing her and reached up to push back a stray hair from her face. His touch sent a fluttering desire through her, but she suppressed it.

He surprised her by pulling her close and kissing her full on the mouth. She deepened the kiss, but only for a moment, not wanting things to go too far too fast. He kissed her forehead and tucked her under his arm with her head resting on his shoulder. She was content to cuddle with him while she listened to his soft breath in the quiet night that mixed with the equally-beautiful sound of Mira's.

Chapter 20

Hannah bolted upright in a half-sleep state when she first heard the creaking of the floorboards. Forcing her eyes open; she first glanced at the sleeping baby in the cradle, as she felt the empty spot next to her in the bed. Daylight had not quite reached the room, but it was enough to see that it was Eli, fully-dressed, toting *two* cups of coffee, who was in the room.

She flopped back down to the mattress, relieved that her instincts were wrong for a change, and there was no reason for her to get up.

Eli sat on the edge of the bed and handed her a cup of coffee with cream—surprisingly, just the way she liked it. She took a sip, wondering if he expected her to help him with chores in the

mornings. She wasn't opposed to helping with gathering the eggs and milking Greta, but she was certainly used to doing much more.

"Did I oversleep?" she asked, taking a sip of the coffee. She could get used to him bringing her coffee.

He climbed in next to her, his shoes already off, and she assumed he left them in the mudroom. She sat up next to him and he opened his arm to her, pulling her close enough to rest her head on his shoulder. This was something she could get used to.

"I was wondering if you'd like to take a sleigh ride with me later."

"A sleigh ride?" she asked jumping from the bed and peering out the window at the thick blanket of snow that had fallen overnight.

She looked back at him. "There must be at least three inches of snow!" she whispered.

"It's more like four," he said. "I had to shovel the walkway for you."

"*Danki.*"

"Will you ask Rachel to watch Mira for about an hour so I can take you for that sleigh ride?"

"Do you think that's a *gut* idea to leave her here alone with Mira when Alana is lurking around?"

"She's gone!" he said, pulling an envelope from his shirt pocket with a smile. "She left a note. Read it for yourself."

Daylight was beginning to seep into the room, and it was just enough light to read the note by. She ran through it quickly, getting to the part where Alana said it was best if she left.

"This is wonderful news," she said loudly, and then hushed herself.

Mira stretched and yawned, causing her parents to smile at one another.

"So what do you say?" he asked. "Will you do me the honor of allowing me to court you properly by going for a sleigh ride with me later?"

"Courting?" she asked. "Are you sure?"

He kissed her lightly on her cheek and then smiled over at Mira and nodded.

"*Jah,* I'm sure!"

THE END

Look for Rachel's Secret: Book Three in this series.

You might also enjoy:

Little Wild Flower: Book One

Hippie-Chick meets Amish guy next door! Jane Abigail Reeves is Little Wild Flower. Raised in the city; Jane and her family move to a farmhouse in a rural Amish community in Indiana as a respite for her alcoholic mother. When she stumbles upon her handsome Amish neighbor, Elijah, she sets out to teach him her big city ways, while he introduces her to the quiet life of the Amish.

Attempting to convert him to her hippie lifestyle, she finds herself drawn to his ways, unable to deny her love for him.

Set in the 1970's, Jane's story is full of cultural obstacles she must overcome in order to put an end to the dysfunction of her family's past.

Can a hippie-chick like Jane find friendship and more with an Amish man, despite their cultural differences?

Little Wild Flower: Book 2

Just when Jane thought her life in the Amish community couldn't get any better, tragedy strikes the Zook farm. Jane suddenly feels lost in the world she created with Elijah, and flees to her home town in search of her childhood friends. Will coming face-to-face with the pain of her childhood send her running back to the farm, or

will she cling to the life she left behind as a teenaged girl?

Little Wild Flower: Book 3

BOOK 3: Little Wild Flower series
When tragedy strikes her brother's family, Jane struggles to find a way to make peace with it all, while managing the growing pains taking place within her own family unit.

When the new doctor turns out to be none other than Bradley, Jane's childhood sweetheart, she struggles

with his new affections, feeling as though she is betraying the memory of her life with Elijah, her deceased husband; the very life that caused her to blend with the Amish community. As she comes to terms with her life without Elijah, she quickly begins to reject some of the Amish traditions, yet keeps others. When she slowly lets go of the life she lost, she discovers that starting over doesn't have to be as difficult as she feared.

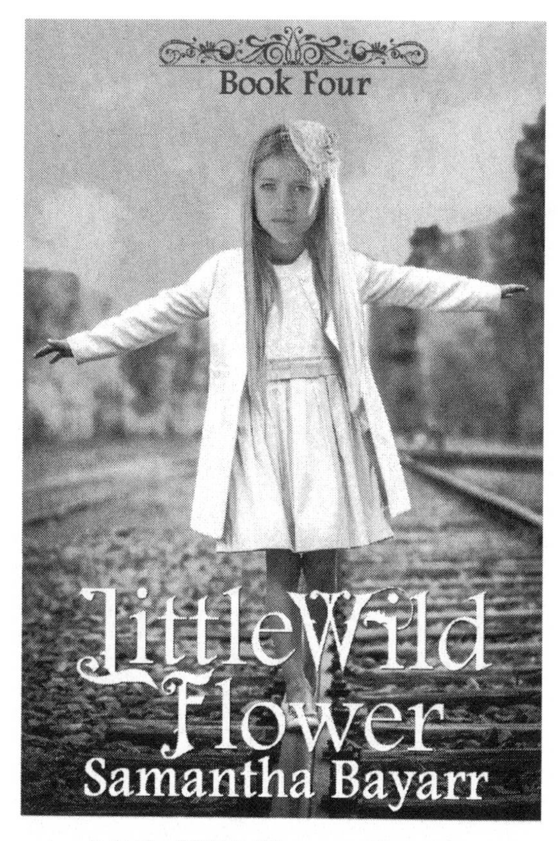

Little Wild Flower: Book 4

Amish Wildflowers continuing story...
All Jane wants is to be a normal child, but she's convinced she needs super-powers to help her survive her tormented childhood at the hands of her alcoholic mother.
By the time she reaches her teen years, Jane is tired of living in fear, feeling she is about to break. When a friend tells her that he believes it's her destiny to save her mother's life--the very person who'd been so cruel to

her, when the opportunity presents itself, Jane doesn't believe she's up to the challenge, since she wishes only the opposite for her mother.
Will she be brave enough to look beyond her own pain and find the strength to save them both, or will Jane become a sacrificial lamb for her mother's sake?

This book contains some mildly disturbing situations in order to maintain the authenticity of the story of Jane's stormy childhood with her alcoholic mother—before she found Jesus and got saved.
Jane's story is based on true events…

Check out these other titles too!

Please LIKE my Facebook Page HERE